THE INTERNAL FRONTIER

CREATING THE
PERSONAL TRANSFORMATIONS
THAT LEAD TO SUCCESS

MORRIS R. SHECHTMAN

NewStar
press

ISBN: 0-7871-8011-4

NewStar Press
a division of NewStar Media Inc.
8955 Beverly Boulevard
Los Angeles, CA 90048

Cover design and digital manipulation by Rick Penn-Kraus
Cover photo of man: Andreas Bleckman/Nonstock
Text design and layout by Hespenheide Design
Printed by Malloy Lithographing, Inc.
Fifth Wave Leadership is a service mark of the Shechtman Institute.

First NewStar Hardcover Printing: October 1998

10 9 8 7 6 5 4 3 2 1

Printed in the United States of America

CONTENTS

To all those courageous individuals who have chosen to look inward; to learn more about themselves; to commit to growth and challenge—to explore the Internal Frontier. Without you, change would grind to a halt, new opportunities would all but disappear, and life would most certainly lose its joy and energy.

INTRODUCTION

This book is about success. More specifically, it's about how you can become more successful than you ever thought possible by looking at what *hasn't* changed in your life. What hasn't changed is the *familiar*, an amazingly strong and persistent drive from childhood that causes you to act, as an adult, in certain predictable ways. We reproduce the *familiar* through all sorts of work behaviors, and while this may help you succeed in certain ways, it can also keep you stuck, frustrated, and unproductive.

My goal is to provide you with the process to identify this *familiar*, let go of the aspects that hurt rather than help, and create new, energizing *familiars*. This process will enable you to achieve your life goals better than any other knowledge or skill you might possess.

A wide variety of people have used this process effectively, and I'm going to share their stories with you. As you'll see, their professional growth was capped until they began dealing with the *familiars* in their lives. Once they began to ask themselves the necessary questions, to "drill down," they experienced breakthroughs at work and in their careers. Drilling down will take you to an emotional level deep enough to find the answers to those questions. In this book I'll show you how to do this. You'll find you can reach a place inside yourself that clarifies behaviors and feelings which, on the surface, are confusing.

Once you've drilled down and identified the *familiar* in your life, you will start distinguishing the inconsequential from the important; you will learn to prioritize expertly, and act decisively. There's an astonishing clarity and power attached to this process. Once you address these personal issues, you will move with much greater assurance and effectiveness through your professional world.

WHAT I'VE LEARNED ABOUT MYSELF

A number of years ago, I made a discovery about myself based on the different jobs that I've held. I've been a therapist, a college professor of literature and cultural history, a consultant to government, law enforcement, and education, and (my current role) a business consultant. Each of these jobs required me to be involved in very different activities; teaching Shakespeare to a bunch of nineteen-year-olds is light-years removed from counseling a middle-aged wife-beater or dealing with a corporate leader's anxiety about downsizing.

At least it's light-years away on the surface. When I drilled down, I discovered that my mission in all of these jobs was the same: to impact people so that their quality of life improved because of what they learned about themselves. My specific job wasn't significant; it was the underlying goal that was important.

People need to get in touch with their underlying goals, with how they feel about what they do. In my life, this discovery has helped me keep clear about what's meaningful and what's trivial. It's given me direction and guided my decision-making. It's helped me become more productive and successful.

As a consultant, I've helped others make similar discoveries about themselves. I've worked with organizations as diverse Binney & Smith (the "Crayola" people), 3M, Northwestern Mutual Life, and Cigna. From chief executive officers to insurance agents to football coaches to government officials, our clients represent a spectrum of personalities and professions. Most of them arrive at our doorstep stymied. They're unhappy with their career progress. They're bored with their jobs. They're overwhelmed by their work responsibilities. They can't adapt to a changing work environment. They're not as successful or effective as they want to be.

Try as they might, they can't figure out what's wrong. That's because they're looking in the wrong places. Typically, they assume that they're stuck because of a stupid boss or ignorant organization; they may believe that they need more training, education, or skills; they may conclude that they just need a change of scenery, and switch jobs or even industries.

What all these people fail to do is link the personal and the professional. Unexamined personal issues from their past are affecting present behaviors. They are being acted upon rather than being actors in their own lives.

If this concept seems like so much psychological mumbo-jumbo, let me clarify what it really is . . . and what it is not. The people I work with aren't seriously disturbed individuals who have repressed some horrific childhood experience. They're not bizarre, pathological people desperately trying to turn around their lives. They are normal men and women who come from typical families—families that have given their members both strengths and issues to work on. Unconsciously, they hurt themselves in work situations because of these unresolved issues.

What they've come to understand—and what this book will help you learn—is that they are engaged in a growth and development process that they control. By becoming "emotionally fit," they can grow and develop at an astonishing pace.

A DOUBLE-EDGED SWORD

Examining your past and identifying recurring patterns of feelings are essential parts of this growth process; they will lead you to your *familiar*. Like many people, you may have certain misconceptions about this process. Misunderstandings abound because of the media's mostly inaccurate stories about psychoanalysis, and because of neurotic therapists who have misused a valuable body of knowledge to foster self-awareness at the expense of action. Their patients don't have the vaguest idea about how to use what they know.

The point of looking into your past is not to place blame or to seek your revenge. Your past issues and emotional baggage aren't simply the result of growing up in dysfunctional, abnormal families. In reality, they're the product of growing up in cultures and subcultures that taught you skills, attitudes, and behaviors appropriate for that time and place but inappropriate for the future. This is no one's fault; this has been true in all eras and cultures. Every generation is enhanced and limited by that to which it becomes accustomed. All of us have a legacy that contains both skills and emotional baggage.

Still, some of you may view looking into your past as dwelling on the negative. I've worked with people who reflexively fight and criticize the process, asserting that nothing good can come from examining the bad things in their lives. If you find yourself reacting this way, understand that this book is your opportunity to come to terms with the whole range of feelings that shapes why you do what you do. These feelings, however, hold the key for you to live a life that is better and more fulfilling.

WAVES AND FRONTIERS

My work as a cultural historian and a psychotherapist has shaped my perspective. I'd like to share some observations related to both these areas that will give you a sense of how this perspective evolved.

Alvin Toffler and other social scientists have talked about the four waves that have produced massive changes in society:

- From hunting and gathering to farming.
- From farming to the Industrial Revolution.
- From the Industrial Revolution to an information-intensive culture.
- From an information-intensive culture to a communication-intensive society.

All these changes required us to adapt. When we evolved to an agricultural society from hunters and gatherers, we realized we didn't have to move around all the time and could settle in one place. When we invented mass production and factories, we discovered we could do more with our lives than subsist and survive. The Internet and other manifestations of the communication revolution have forced us to compete in a global marketplace. All our adapting up to this point has been focused on externals. Now with the Fifth Wave, it becomes internal.

Think about how fast information travels, how quickly new technology spreads. Competitive advantage no longer goes to the first company with the best new product or service. Everything is almost immediately replicable. In an information-intensive world, we've become desensitized to innovation. When scientists discover a new planet with their state-of-the-art telescope, it's a big ho-hum. On an individual level, if you try to acquire the combination of skills that will make you highly marketable, you'll just join the crowd; everyone knows what these skills are because of our information-intensive culture. As soon as career counselors advise young people to focus their efforts on a hot industry, it's no longer hot or there are too many applicants for too few jobs.

In the Fifth Wave, the breakthroughs for both individuals and organizations are internal. The more self-knowledge we have, the better able we'll be to adapt to and capitalize on external forces. Self-aware people don't resist change; they don't make counterproductive decisions based on feelings they don't even realize they have. Instead, they move swiftly and decisively. Self-knowledge is energizing. People who know what drives them are much more willing to take risks, test new ideas, and aggressively pursue opportunities. They're always looking for ways to grow and develop.

For them, the frontiers are internal. They are constantly exploring who they are relative to who they've been. The knowledge they gain gives them an advantage that can no longer be gained through external means.

A FRONTIER THAT'S ACCESSIBLE TO ALL

To capitalize on the ideas in this book, you don't have to spend the next ten years in intensive therapy. Though acquiring self-knowledge and changing behaviors involve some risk and discomfort, everyone is capable of doing so. To help you understand what is involved, I'd like to share the story of one individual we'll call Larry. Throughout this book, I'll be illustrating points with stories of a wide variety of professionals. These are people who have plateaued in their careers or are struggling with different workplace issues. Like Larry, they made no progress on these issues until they turned inward.

Larry is a skilled middle manager in a large technology company who had just received a challenging assignment from his new boss. He was a few weeks into this important project when his boss pulled him off it and gave him another assignment that Larry found mundane. As you might expect, Larry was furious and resentful. Because he wasn't given an explanation as to why he was pulled off the project, he felt excluded and demeaned. Larry, of course, complained to his fellow employees about his supervisor, and a few of them said, "Yeah, the guy has a clique, he plays favorites, we've seen him do this before" and "Get used to it, that's just the way things are."

When we began working with Larry, we told him that his points were valid and we understood why he felt the way he did (though as it turned out, his boss had no idea that Larry was so upset). As we talked to Larry, we asked a simple but revealing question: "Did you go to your boss and tell him how you felt?" Instead of answering the question, Larry went off on a tangent. Later in the discussion, we asked the same question and again he avoided answering directly. When we confronted Larry with his avoidance, he admitted that he hadn't told his boss how he felt. What Larry discovered was that he never told anyone—either at work or in his

personal life—how he felt, in straightforward, unambiguous terms.

Larry's issue isn't unique or even unusual. Like
him, many people are inept when it comes to articulating
their needs. They're often terrific at meeting the needs of
others, but when it comes to their own requirements,
they're speechless and clueless. In fact, Larry "wanted"
to feel like his needs were not being met. As strange as it
may seem, he would have liked nothing better than to
leave the company in a self-righteous furor, feeling like
he worked his tail off but his effort and talents went
unrecognized.

This isn't a conscious process. Larry wasn't aware
that he received a perverse kind of satisfaction from his
martyrdom. He only became aware of his underlying
motivation when it dawned on him that he had played the
same role in his family; there, too, his needs went unmet.
Years later, the power of that role was still exerting itself.

Larry has been making great strides by drilling
down to his personal issues. He's learning how to tell people exactly how he feels and deal with all the anxiety that
action produces. I don't want to pretend this is easy. It
would be far easier for Larry to talk to human resources
about his problem and take a special course on dealing
with difficult bosses; they would help him appreciate
that his boss is under tremendous pressure and Larry
needs to cut him some slack. All this might be true and
easy for Larry to accept, but it has nothing to do with his
real issue. It won't prevent him from turning himself into
a martyr and being stuck with an unrewarding job and a
mediocre career. Unless Larry addresses his core issue,
he's going to find himself trying to reproduce this feeling
of martyrdom time and again.

As you'll see, Larry isn't an anomaly. All of us have feelings we try to reproduce, feelings that prevent us from breaking through to the next level.

A COLLABORATIVE EFFORT

We live in a relationship-driven world, and I would be remiss if I didn't identify three of the relationships that contributed enormously to my work, not to mention this book. Arleah Shechtman, Jim Blackburn, and Rick Kremer are members of the Shechtman Institute, and each of them has taken my ideas and developed them in new directions. Arleah, my wife, is brilliant at exposing core emotional issues faster and more accurately than anyone I've ever worked with. Her ability to cut through surface explanations and issues and figure out what people are struggling with has greatly facilitated my work, as well as my own growth and development.

When I first met Jim, he was a client, very vocal about how useless and ridiculous my concepts were. I've always believed that when an idea resonates for someone, they're either very positive or very negative. Though Jim was vociferously negative at first, he eventually embraced our approach and has been invaluable in creating exercises and activities based on theoretical concepts—exercises and activities that you'll find in the following pages.

Rick, also a former client, has an amazing ability to create structures from these same concepts; he's adept at translating ideas and approaches into formal processes that make sense to people who work in organizations.

I've learned as much from them as they've learned from me, and their contributions will show up on every page of this book. When I refer to work "we" did for different individual and organizational clients in the following pages, Arleah, Jim, and Rick are the colleagues to whom I'm referring.

YOU CAN CHANGE YOUR LIFE BUT YOU CAN'T CHANGE THE WORLD

A few years ago, I wrote a book called *Working Without a Net* that received a great deal of media exposure, largely because Speaker of the House Newt Gingrich held the book up on national television and recommended it to millions of viewers. It focused on how to live and work in a new world that most of us aren't prepared for. The book dealt largely with external changes such as the end of corporate and governmental caretaking, how we were moving from an independent to an interdependent age, the evolving social contract between employers and workers, the disappearance of loyalty, and many other issues.

People who read the book wondered how they could apply the rules to their own lives. How could they respond positively to the realities of a Fifth Wave world? *The Internal Frontier* gives you a process for dealing with these external realities by first changing yourself. Once you've dealt with your internal issues, you are much better able to adapt to the external changes happening all around you.

Many people waste a lot of time and energy trying to change everything but themselves. They change jobs, searching for the perfect employer; they try to transform their bosses and spouses into the people they wish they were; they rail against the unfairness of organizations and of life in general. There's a widespread misconception, especially in affluent Western society, that we have more control over the world than we actually do. Our abundance of technology and wealth creates the illusion that we can control just about everything. Even the most powerful people in our society succumb to this illusion. How many times have governmental leaders vowed not to increase taxes, or CEOs proclaimed they will never downsize, only to discover that they lacked the control they thought they possessed?

Many of us discover that this control is an illusion, and we're overwhelmed by the unpredictability of events. As a result, we become cynical and apathetic. We falsely assume that just because we can't control the world, we can't control our own lives. We figure that there's nothing we can do about it (whatever *it* might be) and say, "Why bother?" Other people choose to become oblivious rather than cynical. In the same way in which members of the counterculture embraced Eastern mysticism in the sixties, we dull our senses and accept whatever happens in our personal and professional lives.

This book offers an alternative to mindless acceptance, cynicism, or beating your head against a wall. No matter which "antidote" you've chosen, I hope the realization that you have tremendous control over your own personal choices proves reinvigorating. It's rejuvenating to realize you can have a powerful impact on everyone you interact with.

In the pages that follow, you'll have the opportunity to reframe your view of who you are and why you do what you do. This is the gateway to change, and if you're able to go through it, the possibilities are endless and enormously exciting.

SELF-DISCOVERY

WHAT YOU'RE LOOKING FOR AND HOW YOU CAN USE IT IN YOUR WORK LIFE

CHAPTER 1

FINDING THE *FAMILIAR*

Since being aware of one's deepest feelings is so important to success in a Fifth Wave world, we all need to identify these feelings relatively quickly and accurately. Just as it helps to have a compass, map, or some other directional tool when exploring new territory, it's essential to have a guide when exploring the Internal Frontier. The process we've developed and tested will serve as that guide.

The process revolves around the *familiar*, a concept I briefly described in the introduction. It's a feeling state we return to again and again, an emotional pattern that has tremendous power over us. Rooted in our family and our upbringing, the *familiar* is a feeling that we unconsciously reproduce. This feeling may cause us not to do things that are productive or smart. It may even cause us to do things that are self-destructive. But our impulse to reproduce the *familiar* is so strong that we do it regardless of the negative behaviors that result.

To demonstrate its power, let's examine an extreme example of the *familiar*. People who have been abused as children often find themselves in abusive relationships as adults. Why does this happen? It's not that they're masochists and consciously seek abusive mates. It's that the feelings engendered by being physically beaten around are so familiar that they short-circuit rational decision-making. When abused children become adults, they reproduce the *familiar* through very different actions. One may end up working for a boss who verbally tortures him and browbeats him mercilessly. Another may join an organization where employees are routinely belittled and devalued. Though these people aren't being physically abused, the feelings produced by this verbal abuse are similar.

Most of the time, however, the *familiar* isn't rooted in an unusual or extreme childhood trauma. The people we work with usually have *familiars* that emerge as part of a relatively normal and healthy childhood. Larry (from the introductory chapter) couldn't tell his boss that he felt demeaned and excluded. Though he grew up with loving parents in a stable family situation, he was the oldest child with many brothers and sisters and often was responsible for taking care of them. On the rare occasions when he would ask his parents for something, they told him he shouldn't be so selfish; as the big brother, he should look out for his younger siblings. Larry's *familiar* was feeling bad about wanting to get his needs met; he had been taught that he was "bad" for wanting anything for himself. Refusing to tell his boss how he felt was only one of many behaviors Larry exhibited to return to this feeling state.

FEELING VERSUS BEHAVIOR

The *familiar* can be a confusing concept at first. We've found that people often struggle to understand that the *familiar* is anchored in feeling, not action. Let's say Joe mistakenly identifies his *familiar* as a behavior such as "working for demanding, highly critical bosses who don't let me make decisions or use initiative." Perhaps Joe has worked for three of these types of bosses and he assumes that this is the *familiar* pattern to which he returns. Joe decides that he's going to break that pattern by finding a job where his boss is mellow, accepting, and nonjudgmental. When he does so, however, Joe is still miserable. He complains that "I never know where I stand with the guy, he's always so vague and never gives me any sense of direction. I feel like I'm being controlled by the new guy as much as I was by the ones who micromanaged me."

"Feel" is the key word. Joe's *familiar* is feeling like someone is controlling his life. His last boss made him feel this way because he didn't help Joe set goals, point out what he's supposed to do, or give him feedback about his performance. Without clear boundaries and goals, Joe feels as out of control as he did in the past. Joe's *familiar* has nothing to do with the type of boss he's drawn to; he's worked for Attila the Hun and Mister Rogers and both make him miserable. To identify the *familiar*, Joe needed to identify the common feeling state.

Working with people like Joe, we never ask them: When have you done that before? If you attempt to locate the *familiar* based on repeated actions, you'll get nowhere. People are ingenious at coming up with new ways to reproduce a *familiar* feeling. As a therapist, I had patients who were divorced four or five times, and they swore they wouldn't make the same mistake after each divorce. That's why they married people who looked and acted very different from each other; they attempted to break the pattern in the same way that Joe did. Unfortunately, all the people they married made them feel the same way, despite their different personalities.

That's why we always ask our clients: When did you *feel* that way before?

Identifying the *familiar* is the first step. The second step, however, isn't to proclaim: "I know that my *familiar* is bad, so from now on I'll do without it." Doing without it is akin to a psychotic break. Your *familiar* is who you are, and you can no more separate yourself from it than you can split yourself in two. *The* familiar *is a very safe place, and it's the only security in an increasingly insecure world.* The second step, therefore, is to create a new, healthier *familiar*. We'll talk about how people can transform their *familiars* a bit later on.

For now, let's look at how a lack of self-knowledge gets people into so much trouble in their professional lives.

THE FLIGHT ATTENDANT AND THE CEO:
TWO *FAMILIAR* STORIES

It was 3 A.M. in Salt Lake City and we were in the middle of what turned out to be an eighteen-hour delay. We got on and got off three different planes, all of which developed mechanical problems that prevented us from leaving the ground. Finally, the airline—one of the majors—gave up and sent us to the customer service area. As you might imagine, it was a chaotic situation as 140 angry, sleep-deprived people descended on the customer service representatives, attempting to secure a room for what was left of the night. After a few hours of restless sleep, we returned to the terminal and boarded yet another plane.

As I boarded, the flight attendant—who was aware of the delay we had experienced—asked how things were going.

"It's been possibly the worst day of my life," I responded.

She recoiled as if I'd slapped her. Then she set herself, put both hands on her hips, and snapped back, "Well, it's not my fault!"

She could not have said anything more destructive and inflammatory at that moment. All I wanted was to communicate my frustration with her airline and have her acknowledge what a nightmare we'd been through. Anything from "I'm sorry for what's happened" to "Yes, I know what you mean, I can't stand all the delays and lack of information myself" would have sufficed.

Why did she act this way? You might answer that she's a typically snotty flight attendant who doesn't care about her passengers. Had I written a letter complaining about her response, as I've done in the past, her superiors would have concluded that she needed more training and would have sent me a form letter and two free-drink coupons. Because they train their flight attendants to say "I'm sorry" in this situation, they would probably think they had to work with her on better empathizing with the customer.

All this is completely wrong. To understand why it's so wrong, consider what would have taken place if I had sent my letter of complaint. The odds are that she would have been questioned by her boss, forced to endure retaliatory training, and been right back at her *familiar*. Think about that *familiar*. Though I don't know this flight attendant, I can make some educated guesses about her. From the outside, it seems like her problem is that she doesn't care enough about her passengers. From the inside, it's the opposite—she cares too much. We've worked with many people in customer service who are like this. Typically, they grow up in an environment where they feel responsible for everyone else's feelings. Because they can't make others feel better, they resent this role. When I told her it was possibly the worst day in my life, she automatically said something that would distance me and make me unhappy because it's beyond her power to make me feel good. Her feelings of helplessness led her to behaviors of which she wasn't conscious.

Her *familiar* is failing to make people happy. Having passengers angry at her, or being reprimanded by her superiors, lets her know exactly who she is. At some point in her life, her deep caring for others became so distorted that it mutated from caring to responsibility—the impossible responsibility of making others feel good about their lives. What she doesn't need is training about how to be more empathetic; if anything, she needs to learn how to be less empathetic.

If we were to work with her, we'd ask her to apologize to a passenger when a similar situation occurs, and remind her that she's accountable for doing so. Then we'd ask her to tell us how she felt about saying she was sorry. While apologizing might be easy for most people, it's a major risk for this flight attendant. To understand the risk, imagine that when this woman was a child, her role was to listen to her mother tell her about how miserable she, the mother, felt. Any deviation from that role would cause her mother to reject her; if she refused to listen, she might not speak to her daughter for the rest of the day. Now think about this little girl approaching her mother and saying, "Mom, I can't do anything about how miserable you feel, so stop telling me about it."

For a child, that's a terrifying (and, of course, impossible) thing to say. For the adult flight attendant, that feeling of terror returns when she has to tell a passenger she's sorry.

A CEO with whom I've worked has different issues from the flight attendant, but he returns to his *familiar* as surely as she does to hers. As the CEO of a highly successful, fast-growth company, George has done extremely well. Smart, hard-working, and savvy about the business world, George has many fine qualities. I was sitting in a meeting with him a while back when he asked me what I thought of the new operations head they recently hired, complaining about all the things this operations person was doing wrong. Though I acknowledged he had some flaws, I also told George that he was the first person in that position who brought stability to operations and was doing a great job.

"But there *is* a major problem in the company," I added.

George immediately snapped to attention, asking what it was.

"You."

I explained to George that he had an obsessive need for struggle and misery, that even when someone was doing a great job he would find fault, aggravate everyone, and disrupt a process that was running smoothly. I also pointed out that he was just waiting for people to disappoint him.

None of this is surprising, given George's tumultuous upbringing. The child of alcoholics, he was thrown out of the house at sixteen and floated around the country, living out of his car and moving from one job to the next. He reproduces that *familiar* feeling of upheaval and abandonment with regularity.

We've worked closely with George on this issue, and he's changing. We've given him behavioral assignments that have paid off in a variety of ways. It used to be that George couldn't sit through a senior-management meeting to save his soul; he'd get up after ten or fifteen minutes and say he had to leave and meet someone, or take control and lead everyone onto some tangential topic—both behaviors relieved his discomfort. George couldn't stand following an agenda and participating in an orderly, organized program. Now, he's able to sit through these meetings and contribute greatly to them.

It's not just young, malleable professionals who are capable of changing. Middle-aged CEOs set in their ways are equally able to transform themselves. The only issue for people who want to change is their ability to tolerate the pain and discomfort of getting to that new place.

STUCK, FRUSTRATED, OVERWHELMED, BORED, AND BLAMING

The pain and discomfort of change are nothing compared to the alternative. We're constantly encountering people who have plateaued, are going nowhere, and don't know how to get unstuck. Irrational fear is rampant in just about every industry and organization—fear of getting fired, of not finding a new job, of losing customers, of receiving a negative performance review, of not advancing quickly enough in one's career. We find many people are overwhelmed by the growing demands placed on them by their organizations or by their professions, law and medicine in particular. Others are bored to tears with jobs that seem to offer no chance for growth and development. There's the sense that "I'm never going to get to the next level; the best I can do is hold on to what I've got."

Breakthroughs don't occur when you go into a shell. They don't take place when you turn cynical or apathetic. They only happen when you go inward and learn how to handle the inevitable disappointments that are part of any professional experience. Self-knowledge keeps people on a growth and development track.

Without that self-knowledge, we get sidetracked by all sorts of unproductive reactions to negative news and events. For instance, many people are enmeshed in blaming their employers. Listen in on the conversations between employees at lunch or after work and you'll hear bitter soliloquies, such as:

> *The company says one thing and does another; they talk about valuing people and they don't; they talk about communicating with us and they don't. How can I do well in a company like this? If they would get their act together, I'd do fine.*

This isn't about the organization; it's about the individual. Organizations teem with contradictions, inefficiencies, and disorder. It's easy for people to seize on these flaws and blame them for their own personal problems. Rather than confronting the personal issues that are preventing them from enjoying the growth and success they desire, they scapegoat the organization.

Most people are not very good at handling disappointment. Instead of using a business setback or customer defection as a catalyst for self-examination and growth, we often become fixated on tangential issues. In our practice, we've worked with many executives who react to disappointment as if it were a personal insult. They can't see that sometimes people make mistakes because they lack the right experience or knowledge or are simply incompetent; they act as if they did it to spite them. "Why did you do this to me?" is their response to a screwup.

Compare this to a sharp middle manager who had completed one of our programs. Each year, her company invites its top performers to an annual meeting. The previous year, she was invited; this year, she was not. When she approached us about this situation, we expected hostility and recriminations. She might have complained that she didn't butter up the boss or that many people were chosen who shouldn't be going. Instead, she said she was disappointed and angry, but that she was OK with those feelings. She recognized that she had to work on improving her performance so that she would be chosen next year. Rather than squandering her energy on things outside herself and outside her control, she concentrated on internal issues.

She was able to do this because she had identified the *familiar* pattern to which she used to return and was skilled at creating new, healthier *familiars*, based on her experiences in our program. Most people don't do this. Instead, they become fearful about losing something they've gained. Drilling down is the only way to get beyond this fear. Often someone gives us a description of some cataclysmic event. A lawyer tells us that the firm is putting tremendous pressure on him to bring in new clients and he's worried that he can't do it. An accountant is terrified that her firm will be acquired and she'll lose her job.

We always respond to these apocalyptic descriptions with: Why is that a problem?

People usually say it's a problem because they're afraid they'll be fired or suffer a loss of income or be chewed out by a superior.

Again we ask: Why is that a problem? Do you feel no one else will hire you? Do you think you'll never be able to boost your income?

All these questions come down to issues of self-confidence and self-esteem. What I refer to as self-confidence and self-esteem is really the ability to get one's needs met and believe that this is a legitimate pursuit. Some people have such low expectations for themselves that they cling to what they have (a job, an income level, a company or practice they built) like a life preserver. These people grew up in families that rigidly adhered to empty routines. No one ever challenged anyone, no one ever connected with each other on a real feeling level. Instead, they subordinated feelings to the routine—they'd go to church every Sunday and Grandma's house on Friday, talk about the same mundane matters every night at dinner, and so on. As adults, these people view change as threatening. They return to the familiar feeling of emptiness and aloneness where there are no surprises. The prospect of losing one's job, therefore, is scary. Sometimes this fear is laughably irrational. There are vested middle managers in high-growth companies terrified of being downsized, who will receive millions of dollars if they're let go. They can't possibly believe they and their families will starve. Unless they're woefully incompetent, they'll eventually find other jobs. Their fears are rooted in familiar feelings that were ingrained when they were children. As a result, they make decisions at work based on fear (doing nothing that might earn them a negative mark) rather than a desire to excel.

FACING PAINFUL REALITIES

A certain amount of discomfort comes with this drilling-down process. Many people have lived for years with what they wanted to believe about themselves rather than the truth. It hurts to realize that you plateaued years ago and haven't gone anywhere since, or that you're incapable of articulating your own needs. Letting go of a comfortable *familiar* and creating a new one demands a certain amount of fortitude.

That is especially difficult because of societal attitudes and stereotypical notions of all kinds. Instead of drilling down, we drill sideways. Society has given minorities of all kinds socially acceptable ways of distracting themselves from the real issues. For example, political correctness, our view of addictions as a disease, and the prevailing perspective on poverty all give license to avoid choices and responsibility. But it's not only minorities. White male managers are equally distracted by notions of how and when they should confront employees.

Our culture encourages individuals with problems to defer to group attitudes, and sends them the message that they can blame their individual failure on bias and pigheadedness. People use the group as a way to avoid looking at themselves. Certainly prejudice and narrow-mindedness still exist throughout our culture, and it is everyone's responsibility to confront and end it. Prejudice is not only anathema from a moral perspective, but it produces ineffective workers and managers. Bigotry is a result of arrested development, and we work with bigots in the same way that we work with other employees who have developmental deficits. Consider a white manager who believes that his entry-level Hispanic workers are not bright enough to go into management. This white manager doesn't feel that way because he's ignorant about Hispanic culture or needs more interaction with minorities. Instead, he's suffering from personal opaqueness; he is clueless about the fear-driven and choiceless world he has created for himself, and Hispanics (or any other available group) are an easy distraction for his anxiety.

At the same time, we regularly encounter companies where entry-level minority workers use their minority status to manipulate management and create an environment of chronic mistrust and low morale. They cling to the belief that "white management" (many of whom often are not white) has lied to them, is lying to them, and will always lie to them regardless of evidence to the contrary. Believing that someone always has your worst interests at heart is a lot less painful than facing the fact that the people you depended on early in your life gave you a raw deal. Group mythologies will always be preferable to dealing with one's own history and pain. That's why diversity programs, which simply attack superficial symptoms, help managers avoid confronting dysfunctional and destructive individuals.

Political correctness and "protective" legislation also prevent organizations from confronting people who refuse to deal with their personal issues. There's a smart, skilled woman we've worked with who acts calm and demure when she's actually furious. She would sit primly during meetings, smile at everyone, and never criticize anyone or utter a negative word, even when she believed the group was making an idiotic decision. As a result, no one knew that she was disappointed or angry until after the fact, when she might mention that she was really bothered by what someone said or what a team did. Because she's so insightful and talented, it would be valuable for everyone if she expressed her disappointment when she felt it; better decisions would be made if she made her feelings known.

For years, however, no one confronted her about her behavior. In many ways, she was conforming to a traditional female role within organizations. No one felt comfortable asking her why she was being so "ladylike" or suggesting that she would be more effective if she was more direct and forceful. Gender roles are touchy subjects, and nobody wanted to touch this one.

When I learned what was going on, I asked her, "Have you ever told any men you work with that you were angry or disappointed?" This was a difficult question for me to ask; it made her uncomfortable as well. But it allowed her to speak the unspoken truth; it gave her an opening to talk about issues from her past. As it turned out, she'd been sent the message while growing up that "good girls" kept their feelings to themselves, and her busy dad made it clear he didn't want to deal with her messy feelings. Just talking about these issues started her on an internal path, and through the work she's done she's now much better able to express her feelings directly and at appropriate times.

"FIND THE *FAMILIAR*" EXERCISE

The *familiar* can be a confusing concept. Typically when I work with people, they often mistakenly assume that their *familiar* is a repeated behavior or a secondary emotion. It takes a while not only to understand the concept but to drill down far enough into yourself and your past to reach that familiar feeling.

Throughout this book, I'll provide advice and techniques to identify the *familiar*. The purpose of this exercise is to let you practice looking for the *familiar* that's impacting the performance of the two people in the following stories:

1. The only son of a military father and a mother who was a nurse, Doug grew up while moving from town to town. Despite the movement, his upbringing was "normal" in many respects. His father was strict but fair, and his mother was compassionate and warm. Unfortunately, they weren't around much; his father spent a great deal of time on assignment and would be gone for weeks or even months, and his mother's nursing schedule often forced her to work odd hours.

As a child, Doug spent a great deal of time with his father's mother, who lived with the family. Grandma Liz was a demanding, high-energy woman. She constantly pushed Doug to do better. If he received a B in school, she would ask why not an A; if he received an A, she would ask why not an A+. Grandma Liz was a highly critical woman who found fault with Doug constantly. Though he was not a troublesome or ill-mannered child, she frequently admonished him for the way he made his bed, for his choice of clothes, and for how he sometimes wasn't as polite as she thought he should be.

Doug was a solid student and majored in business in college, and then earned his MBA. He joined a large packaged-goods company as an assistant brand manager, but he quickly got into trouble with his boss because he kept missing deadlines by a day or two. Though the quality of his work was high, he never seemed able to meet the deadlines his boss set. Because of a less-than-glowing performance review, Doug found another job with a boss who was not as rigid about deadlines as his former boss. Though Doug received praise for his marketing expertise and creative contributions, his boss disliked Doug's casual reporting style; Doug would turn in reports that were often disorganized and poorly written. His boss valued Doug's contributions and tried to get him to improve his report-writing, but though Doug promised he'd try, he didn't make much progress. After two incidents in which Doug's sloppy reports resulted in missed opportunities, Doug was let go.

Doug's *familiar* is:

    A. Choosing bosses with whom he's incompatible.

    B. Considering himself superior to whatever job he has (and thus ignoring tasks or rules he feels are beneath him).

    C. Deliberately making mistakes so that he can leave boring jobs.

    D. Feeling sad that he can't please others no matter what he does.

The correct answer is D. A and C are behaviors, B is an intellectual activity, and the *familiar* is always a feeling. When Doug sabotages himself with easily correctable mistakes, he reproduces a situation of never being able to please others. His feeling is sadness. Doug felt sad growing up when he couldn't satisfy his grandmother's expectations; now he feels sad when his bosses express their disappointment in his efforts. Feeling sad because he doesn't measure up isn't a good feeling, but it's one that's *familiar*; Doug knows exactly who he is when he's sad about falling short of the mark.

2. Tina grew up in a very affluent home in an exclusive New York suburb. Her father was a highly successful surgeon and her mother was renowned for her volunteer work. Tina was spoiled by her parents, especially her father. He showered her with presents and praised everything she did. He would rarely reprimand her, no matter how egregiously obnoxious her behavior might be. At the same time, it was equally rare for her father to express to Tina how he really felt about anything or listen to how she felt. For instance, Tina's best friend moved away when she was eight years old, and she tried to tell her father how sad she was. But as soon as he saw her sad face and she started to talk about her friend leaving, he "jollied" her out of her bad mood, taking her out for ice cream and promising her a trip to the zoo as soon as the weather turned warmer.

Tina went to law school, made Law Review, and was recruited by a top New York firm. With her amazing memory and ability to reason out solutions to complex problems quickly, she was viewed as a rising star at the firm. After nine years there, however, she still hadn't made partner. The problem was her people skills, or so the partner to whom she reported explained. Not only did Tina tend to bully paralegals and secretaries, but she was seen by clients as cold and even disdainful.

In addition, though many of the partners greatly admired her skills, none of them was willing to mentor her. In fact, she had no close relationships with anyone at the firm. Upset that she wasn't viewed as "partner material," Tina blamed her boss and other male partners for excluding "smart" women, believing that the other women who had been made partners were promoted because they were willing "to play the game."

Tina's *familiar* is:

    A. Feeling bitter and angry that her skills aren't rewarded.

    B. Feeling abandoned and isolated.

    C. Considering herself smarter than everyone else.

    D. Feeling frustrated because she refuses to play politics.

The correct answer is B. While the other answers may be correct in the sense that she often is angry, bitter, frustrated, and smug about her abilities, they don't drill down far enough. Her anger, for instance, is a secondary emotion. Abandonment and isolation are the core of her feelings. All those years that her father never expressed his feelings to her or acknowledged her feelings created a terrible loneliness inside Tina. She can re-create that isolation by refusing to form meaningful relationships with other people at the law firm and with clients; she pushes them away with her bullying behavior and disdainful attitude.

A BIG DIFFERENCE

As you've probably gathered by now, our approach is significantly different from what you've been exposed to at work or in private therapy. It doesn't simply help you learn more about yourself or acquire new skills. It doesn't only function on a behavioral level. What it does do is drill down to a feeling level and help you change.

Many of us do weird, ineffective, and self-destructive things in our work lives, and as a result we are funneled into training, see a coach, or go into therapy. What's different about our approach is that it helps people figure out where this behavior comes from, why they're compelled to do things they'd rather not do (or have no knowledge that they're doing) and make positive and often dramatic changes in their lives by identifying the *familiar* and creating new *familiars*.

On the surface, it may seem that therapy and training achieve similar goals. Let's take a moment and examine the surface similarities. Training is based on the premise that if you change people's thinking, you'll change their feelings and thus their behaviors. Everything I've learned tells us that you can't change their thinking (and thus their behaviors) if you don't address their feelings first. Training is a massive exercise in intellectual analysis, leaving trainees with a better understanding of why they're screwed up but with very little motivation or tools to change. Trainers use all sorts of devices to convey how to do something differently, how to be more effective, how to communicate better, how to manage conflict, and so on. No one, however, factors in the personal issues of trainees and helps them deal with these issues in work situations.

Therapy, as practiced by private therapists or corporate coaches in the form of counseling, does penetrate to people's feelings, and you learn a great deal about the source of your anger or the cause of your anxiety. But there's no accountability that follows, or a way to transfer what you've learned to a work environment. By accountability, I mean that people can't just talk about wanting to change; they have to do it or else. As a therapist, I committed heresy by holding my patients accountable. Spouse and drug abusers would come in to see me and say they needed help to stop beating their wives or using drugs. I would say, "Fine, but you have to stop that behavior before I'll treat you, and if I receive any indication that you resumed it, I will never see you again." At that point, they'd protest, "No, no, you don't understand, that's what I need help with." And I'd respond that *they* didn't understand; they needed to make a choice, and I was going to hold them accountable for it.

Therapists are trained to accept people for who they are, and to view their role as essentially passive and noninterfering (in "real" events of their patients' lives). As a result, many people spend years in therapy acquiring great insights into why they do the things they do, but remain unable to apply what they've learned to their lives. It's no coincidence that the only successful personal-growth programs are those that are ruthless in their accountability. Alcoholics Anonymous, for instance, involves a relationship between alcoholic and sponsor that is one of unbending expectations and no excuses. If you make a commitment to the sponsor and fail to deliver, the sponsor is empowered and held accountable for putting this relationship at risk or ending it. AA expects you to be accountable, and if you're not, they want nothing to do with you.

When you look at therapy and training from this perspective, you realize that they both treat people as if they're incapable of dealing with their feelings. The patronizing attitude that underlies both therapy and training ultimately sabotages people's growth and development.

The ruthless accountability that's central to our approach is probably very different from anything you've been exposed to. We require evidence that people are willing to engage in a process of change, a process where they're continually taking risks. If you want to change, you have to do things that scare you. It's not giving up the pleasures of the drug that scares cocaine users; it's that without the drug, they have to deal directly with their feelings. The process of creating a new *familiar* causes people to tackle some very difficult feelings head-on, and we don't let people get away with avoiding this task.

Why do all this? You might be asking yourself if you really have to change. Perhaps you know other people who never changed jobs or took on new challenges and were successful at what they did. In the past, it was possible to avoid change and growth and do OK. The bar, however, has been raised, and it gets higher and higher every day. In the world in which we live, everyone (or so it sometimes seems) has an MBA; everyone has immediate access to cutting-edge data and technology; everyone knows how to network. To move forward in your career and be more effective in your work, you can no longer look outside yourself for an edge. Having the right degree, working hard, and keeping up with the latest developments in your field simply allows you to compete in your given arena. To get ahead and increase your effectiveness, you need to change and grow. People who are willing to confront problematic behaviors and trace them back to their emotional source will adapt and evolve much faster than others. They don't retreat into a shell when their company is taken over or become stuck in battles over trivial matters with a new boss. They learn how to make faster decisions because they're clear about who they are, and that clarity provides the confidence necessary for fast decision-making. They become master relationship builders because they're open and vulnerable, willing to take the risks necessary to form productive relationships.

In other words, they possess the internal awareness required to change and grow in ways that not only increase their productivity but enhance their marketability. In a Fifth Wave world, these are attributes to be prized.

CHAPTER 2

WHY THE CULTURE DEMANDS PERSONAL TRANSFORMATION

To get ahead and become better at our work, people used to acquire new skills and knowledge. Teachers went back to school for advanced degrees; business people signed up for special training; doctors attended conferences where they could learn about innovative techniques and procedures. The notion was that if they could only obtain this cutting-edge skill or that critical new area of knowledge, they would greatly increase their effectiveness and career prospects.

It's not that skills and knowledge have ceased to be important. It's that they're now just the ante to play the game. In the Fifth Wave, we're moving from the age of information and communication to an era of self-knowledge. The data and skills you've gained are only useful to the extent that you know who you are and where you want to go. Without that self-knowledge, all the information in the world won't do you much good.

The Fifth Wave challenge for both individuals and organizations is to connect knowledge to self-growth.

HOW THE CULTURE IS PUSHING US INWARD

An executive with a high-tech company was telling me about how it had come up with a marvelous innovation for computer-chip design, one that was a clear and significant improvement over past chip designs. He added that no one at his organization was particularly excited about this innovation, however, since it was quickly and effectively copied by competitors. "As good as our technical people are, they don't give us much of an edge these days," he explained. "Our success comes from building relationships, not products."

Everywhere you look, you see this scenario repeated. Financial advisers used to provide their clients with information designed to manage their investments. Today, the savvy consumer knows as much as (and sometimes more than) the adviser—there's an enormous amount of easy-to-understand, accessible information available about the best funds, diversification strategies, and so on. If advisers want to keep their clients, they need to apply that information to clients' goals and life situations. To do that, advisers must be able to understand and communicate with clients in deeply personal ways. In other words, they must establish real relationships with them, as opposed to the superficial "business" relationships of the past.

It's difficult to build this type of relationship if you're constantly returning to old *familiars*. They spawn behaviors that close you off to others and hamper communication. As a result, you have a diminished capacity for building intimacy and connectedness. The evidence for this relationship-building trend is overwhelming. Think about how salespeople used to be trained. For years, organizations told salespeople that they needed to entertain prospects and customers, give them lots of information, and take orders. Now their customers can obtain the same information from the Internet, and all their schmoozing skills have left them desperately chasing shaky transactions with an increasingly migratory clientele. Salespeople in every industry are struggling to make the transition from turning short-term profits into sustainable profitability. They, like people in many other professions, are still focused on external survival rather than internal growth. They just want to get by; their most optimistic goal is to escape downsizing rather than to grow and develop.

Most of us have been raised in a survival-oriented paradigm, and we're having trouble making the shift to what is an increasingly growth-oriented environment. For many people, survival means doing just enough to get by. It's disturbing to go after more and to take the risks that growth entails.

This survival mentality is a critical part of our biological and social history. We're programmed to move toward entropy as well as growth. As humans, we have this odd drive to do contradictory things. People who return to their old *familiar* are driven by entropy, and people who establish new, healthier *familiars* are driven by growth. Everyone has both drives, and the challenge is to act on growth more than entropy. We all can choose between being slugs or peak performers. It shouldn't come as a surprise that many people choose the former, since inertia is a natural animal state. Lions don't spend their time exploring new territory and searching for new rivals to conquer; they kill an animal, eat it, and then sleep for the entire day. While people are a bit more energetic and a bit less rapacious, we're still not all that far removed from this impulse toward inertia. We know how exhausting dealing with growth issues can be, especially if we're parents. Healthy, growing children never stop challenging the status quo, and parents don't get up in the morning eager to deal with lots of "why can't I do this" questions. It's much easier to deal with passive children who are habitually compliant and accept whatever you say.

There's always been a tension between our conditioned movement toward inertia and our excitement about the opportunities growth presents. Prior to the information revolution, growth played a different role in our lives. It was more predictable, more external, and driven more toward an end than a process. It was in essence geared more toward well-heeled survival than it was toward continual challenge. Now, however, we no longer can err on the side of survival and deny the challenges in growth. Though growth may seem the logical choice intellectually, it's a big emotional leap.

Many Americans, for instance, are not far removed from ancestors whose belief systems were indelibly shaped by deprivation and fear in our own country or in the land of their birth. They have grandparents or parents who were raised in societies dominated by poverty, brutality, and hopelessness. Their fear that they could lose everything they'd worked for in one capricious moment was absolutely realistic. This terror has been handed down from generation to generation. It has little to do with current reality but a lot to do with the historical *familiar*. There's no doubt that in our contemporary environment, change can descend with disorienting suddenness. While horrific events from the past had a greater hold on previous generations, we continue to see reactions driven more by demons from the past than harbingers of the future. For instance, people's fear of losing their jobs is more appropriate for a new immigrant than an experienced professional. We've heard countless people tell us in trembling tones, "If I lose this job, it's all over for me." Why? Will someone come and confiscate all your possessions? Will you be executed? Contrast this survival orientation with the following growth perspective:

I'd be sad and disappointed if I were to lose this job, but the job is not who I am. As someone who is growing and developing, there will be other opportunities out there for me, and I'll find a new and different job.

Organizations, unfortunately, usually don't foster this healthier attitude. Their reactions to both disaffected employees and unhappy customers are driven by panic and a mind-set of scarcity. Companies make an extraordinary effort to mollify and pacify, trying to extinguish disappointment and the threat they feel it poses to survival. Growth-driven businesses, on the other hand, recognize that disappointment goes with the territory because all relationships at one time or another are disappointing. At various times, employees don't like their employers, employers don't like their employees, customers don't like their suppliers, and suppliers don't like their customers. In a survival organization, disappointment is cataclysmic; in a growth organization, disappointment is a new beginning.

A HEALTHY CHOICE

Instead of hunkering down and trying to hold on to everything we've gained, we can choose to grow. Growth is not getting more of something. In years past, people felt they were "growing" if they were acquiring more money, more security, more friends, more hobbies. But growth isn't about more; it's about new. It's not about the repetition of the same experience; it's about living for new experiences. Given the rapid pace of change, there are more new experiences and opportunities to be had than at any time in our history. We need the stimulation these experiences provide. Studies show that children who aren't stimulated suffer from "failure-to-thrive" syndrome. Adults have the same need, and they receive no stimulation from performing the same task or using the same skill over and over.

Nevertheless, people still choose to stay in the same job far too long. The old cultural model was: If you're good at something, keep doing it. Today, people plateau in their jobs and remain doing the same thing for months or even years after they should have left. One of our clients, on the other hand, hires people he refers to as "players." These are people who have explored their internal frontiers, who relish learning new things and moving from position to position. When they master a skill, players move on to something new.

You're going to be seeing more players emerging in all sorts of fields. Doctors, for instance, are not only confronted with an avalanche of new research and techniques, but they have to cope with HMOs, alternative medicine, and a wide variety of other forces. If they don't respond to the challenge of what's new and continuously change the way they work, they're going to have problems.

Of course, people can choose to resist what's new, and then complain about working more and earning less than ever before. There are many professionals who cling to their jobs, convinced that if they lose those jobs, they too will be lost. "Who else is going to pay me as much as

I'm making now?" they ask. No one will. In today's world, if you do what you've always done, your income is now guaranteed to diminish each year. If you make changes in who you are, however, you give yourself an excellent chance to make more money than you've ever made before.

I've seen people in high-tech companies with multiple doctorates who refuse to make internal changes. They're brilliant people with tremendous academic backgrounds making $10 an hour on a high-tech assembly line. We ask them:

- *Why are you afraid to build new relationships?*
- *What are your fears about articulating your needs to people?*
- *What are your fears about making demands on people close to you?*

Typically, they respond that they're not up to doing the things others do and are content to stay at their current level. They talk about how other people are "nervy" and "pushy" and "obnoxiously aggressive." They prefer to be laid-back and passive rather than work hard at building bridges to the right people in the organization. The notion of changing who they are seems impossible: "I wasn't raised that way." This stance returns them to their *familiar: To hope for what they can never obtain.*

Like these high-tech Ph.D.s, you are confronted with choices. You can choose to withdraw as they did and blame others for your failures. Or you can face your internal demons and grow like crazy. Asking yourself the three "fear" questions will increase the odds that you choose the latter rather than the former.

THE PAST STILL HAUNTS US

Until relatively recently, you could have avoided facing these demons. Before the information and communication revolutions, the pressure of change and choice was less intense. People might be poor relationship builders, for instance, but be able to maintain customers who demanded very little beyond basic information and good products and services from their suppliers.

It's a mistake, however, to think that these personal demons didn't exist years ago; it's just that circumstances didn't demand that we confront them. My grandmother, for instance, was a very bright and talented seamstress who took one menial job after the next. Unable to tell her employers what she needed, she resorted to bitter complaints—to us, not them—about being exploited. We asked her why she didn't do anything about it, and she simply sighed and said that if she did, she would be fired. My grandmother modeled the terror of reaching out and going after what she wanted in life. In her experience in Russia, people literally got killed for asserting themselves. Though things were different in this country, the fear was too close and too real for her to deal with her feelings.

Even though these events took place many years ago, they still affect us today. My grandmother taught me and my siblings that we would only go so far because we were Jews and would run into prejudice everywhere. When we would tell her that we weren't running into it, she'd say, "Just wait, you will." I understand and appreciate this; it was based on very real and very awful experiences and this legacy has continued in succeeding generations through the belief system that says, "No matter how good it gets, sooner or later the other shoe will drop."

Our *familiars* are not all bad. They usually leave us with tools and skills that take us to a certain level of success. One of the positives of my grandmother's legacy, for instance, is that I'm adept at articulating my positions because I was always expecting to get shot down based on who I was. At the same time, it left me some baggage: *When I raise my expectations and achieve something, I wonder if I deserve it; I am the Jew who will get what he's achieved taken from him.* By my being conscious of this legacy and wrestling with it, its power over me lessens.

All groups—economic, generational, ethnic, and so on—are impacted by past events. The generation raised during the Depression learned to be happy with what they had and to be grateful just to be alive. Many members of this generation have passed this lesson on, knowingly or not, to their children. Unexamined and undealt with, the *familiars* spawned by past generational messages become governors on any future growth and development. In a time of rapid change and escalating demands, they produce a self-destructive regression into victimization and helplessness. Our times have profoundly raised expectations for individuals and organizations. "Grow or die" is a singularly meaningful phrase in this perpetually challenging world.

IN THE FIFTH WAVE, THERE'S NO ONE TO BLAME BUT YOURSELF

The most difficult risk for people to take today is to overcome their history. The financial risk that entrepreneurs take is nothing compared to interpersonal risk. This risk has not only familial but social roots. Individuals who are members of historically disenfranchised groups, for instance, continue to use disenfranchisement as an excuse for their failures instead of facing their *familiars*. It takes guts to ignore everything your past has taught you, and feel that you're entitled to meet your needs. It requires great courage not to rely on external excuses for why you haven't achieved your goals.

The Fifth Wave has made victimization less viable. In the past, we could legitimately blame racism, sexism, ageism, and a variety of other societal evils for our plight. While vestiges of discrimination remain, the combined might of information and communication demonstrate to everyone that our society has opened up to an extraordinary degree. You'd have to be living in a cave to be unaware that women, blacks, and other minorities enjoy greatly increased power and influence in today's society. Similarly, organizations are much more likely to promote people based on their ability to generate results rather than on their social pedigree, academic degrees, or membership in old-boy networks. It would be financial suicide in today's intensely competitive environment to do otherwise. Anyone opening a business magazine will read about entrepreneurs who have been hugely successful even though they lacked the right training and social graces. This widespread awareness of an increasingly open society causes us to look inward: If *they* aren't causing our problems, the only one left is *us*.

Some people still get sidetracked from their personal issues by other excuses. "He was in the right place at the right time" and "It's who you know that counts" are two common ones. They ascribe the success of others to the mysterious hand of fate. It's comforting to believe that success is just something that happens to the lucky few. If we embrace this belief, we don't have to deal with the painful realities of why we're not among them. A friend and a client who's a leader in the insurance field has a saying: "Successful insurance agents do what unsuccessful agents are unwilling to do." What they do is examine their internal issues so that they can place themselves in the right place at the right time and get to meet the right people in order to build the right relationships.

We avoid this self-examination by refusing to give people their due. Success-bashing is everywhere in our culture. It's great camouflage for our willingness to settle for who we are rather than who we might become. It's very painful to admit that we've chosen to be mediocre. We're especially likely to gravitate toward success-bashing in an era that makes everyone aware of the many powerful options we can choose to change our lives.

The debate in our culture over "leveling the playing field" represents desperate attempts to disguise choices that keep people mired in their *familiar*. Every day throughout our society, courageous people take huge leaps of faith and leave their *familiar* behind to embrace something new, unfamiliar, and scary. They move beyond lousy housing, poor schools, disorganized families, and dangerous neighborhoods, and initiate relationships they were once taught to believe were not for them.

Success is largely driven by our expectations and willingness to change. In an open Fifth Wave society, everyone can choose to be successful. That doesn't mean that it's as easy for someone who grew up poor to succeed as it is for someone who had many material, social, and educational advantages. What it does mean, however, is that in our current culture, the real advantage is internal rather than external; no one is born with a natural talent for change. All of us—rich and poor alike—are given issues by our families that inhibit our ability to change. In today's world, however, there is more incentive than ever before to deal with these issues. Success is available to anyone who is brave enough to face who he is beneath the surface; if he takes that risk, he can change with great speed and flexibility.

Unfortunately, many of us are choosing to remain the same. When people focus on the external issues—on bashing the successful and demanding equal playing fields—it demonstrates their fear of facing their own internal issues and taking the risk that comes with change.

THE INSIGHTS AND SKILLS THAT LEAD TO SUCCESS

Aren't there successful people who commit the sins of blaming and success-bashing? Even in our Fifth Wave era, aren't there people who have no concept of their *familiars* but have managed to do just fine?

Of course. The problem is that sooner or later, their failure to explore their internal frontiers will land them in trouble. Still, some measure of success is possible for these people because most family experiences send a mixture of healthy and neurotic messages:

- *Message No.1: We're not interested in your needs; don't come to us with those needs.*
- *Message No. 2: Don't let anyone stand in your way of getting what you want because you can do whatever you want to do.*

I know a CEO whose parents literally and figuratively abandoned him. As a result, he finds it difficult as an adult to achieve the type of intimacy necessary for building relationships. On the other hand, the man's father taught him that he shouldn't settle and that he should never, ever take any guff from anyone. The only way this CEO survived his family was by depending on no one but himself.

It's not surprising, therefore, that he had the drive and determination to build an organization by himself. It also shouldn't be surprising that now that the organization employs 20,000 people, he's running into all sorts of problems. He can no longer intuitively run a company this size. He needs to rely on others to build relationships, and it's very difficult for him to trust others sufficiently to do so.

Even if our parents didn't abandon us and we grew up in relatively normal families, we still have to identify the mixed messages we received. Once we're aware of the strengths and challenges our upbringing left us with, we're in a much better position to capitalize on those strengths and meet those challenges. It's important to be aware of them for many reasons, not the least of which is that an asset can turn into a liability. In his twenties when he was building his company, the man's fierce individualism was an asset; it became a liability in his forties when he was trying to manage a huge organization.

When my colleagues and I help people explore their internal frontiers and discover things about themselves based on their family experiences, we give them the opportunity to develop a skill that is absolutely essential for success in the Fifth Wave. Relationship-building is something I've alluded to earlier and will examine in greater detail later on. For now, it's important to understand that relationship-building is based on two prerequisites: the ability to engage in conflict and the ability to self-disclose. Without self-knowledge, these prerequisites are unattainable. Only when you've explored who you are do you trust yourself enough to extend that trust to others. That's what self-disclosure is all about, and it's one of the cornerstones of relationships.

Most highly successful people we work with have superior relationship-building skills. One aspect of this skill is that they're surprisingly open about who they are—surprising to the people who work for and with them. As one of our clients put it:

I'm amazed that John doesn't try to act like a boss in front of me. There's no secret agenda with him; I know exactly where he's coming from. John doesn't have to "pull power" on me. I do things for him because of the influence he has on me because of our relationship. It's not that John never gets upset about some things, and he lets me know it. But that's the key. Whether he's happy or angry, he's very direct in expressing how he feels. I know he would never do anything behind my back, and that's why I trust him as much as he trusts me.

This is the model for relationship-building now and in the future. Whether you're a businessperson, doctor, lawyer, or any other type of professional, you know customers, patients, and clients have many solid "technicians" to choose from. Simple technical competence or even brilliance doesn't guarantee loyalty anymore. All it does is ensure that you may have one or more transactions. People need to experience the application of that knowledge to their lives in a deeply personal and meaningful way. That can only be accomplished in a relationship infused with trust, and that trust only comes when *both* people are open and vulnerable. If you're able to build strong relationships based on trust, you gain a crucial competitive edge.

I depend on a health-care professional to treat some long-standing problems that can interfere with my schedule and lifestyle. About seven years ago, he opened up to me and confessed that he'd been a cocaine addict for most of his adult life. When he told me this, I confronted him about what he was going to do about it, and after our discussion, he shut down his practice for a year and went to a recovery center. I could have found other specialists at this point. His expertise—which had been somewhat unusual when I first started seeing him—was now readily available. But I stuck with him because he was open and vulnerable with me, and I trust him implicitly. He's been clean for the past six years, and I haven't had any reason to regret my decision.

AN ONGOING CHALLENGE

All these issues aren't going to disappear. Sometimes people will wishfully wonder if our current intensely competitive, information-driven culture is only a temporary aberration, and that at some point soon we'll return to an earlier era where people have jobs for life, where we don't have to take a global marketplace into consideration, where we don't have to work harder and longer than ever before. This is a pipe dream. Short of a cataclysmic world event that shuts down the flow of information, the stakes will continue to rise. Information boosts our expectations; it keeps pushing us toward higher standards of performance. Individuals and organizations are bombarded with so much information that leads to so many opportunities, it's impossible to resist them. Though some of us may struggle with our inertia and refuse to make the personal changes necessary to keep up with the world around us, others will set the pace by readily identifying old *familiars* and creating new ones.

I should add that they'll go through this process not once, but many times. One of the biggest mistakes people in therapy make is to say: "Oh, I dealt with that issue, it's over." The *familiar* is a lifelong issue. In this Fifth Wave world of ours, we're always going to have to grapple with the hold our particular *familiar* has on us. That doesn't mean it has to be this awful struggle each time. Many people we work with learn how to be creative in articulating their issues; they treat their work with the *familiar* as a healthy activity and even have a sense of humor about it.

In one way, the *familiar* is like any significant loss; you never completely get over it because it's a part of your history. As long as you're aware of it and working on it, its power over your behaviors will diminish. By risking behaviors that don't reproduce that old familiar feeling, you can make all sorts of breakthroughs in your personal and professional life. I know many highly successful people from humble beginnings who feel inadequate and diminished whenever they deal with powerbrokers. No matter how much they've achieved in their lives, they feel ashamed of who they are when they work with powerful decision makers and leaders who attended prestigious schools and work for Fortune 100 companies. Accepting that they're always going to wrestle with these feelings is one of the healthiest things they can do. Risking behaviors that don't reproduce these feelings will help them find and capitalize on opportunities that others can only dream about. The people who continuously meet this challenge of acceptance and risk will be the ones who break through to the next level in their organizations and careers.

CHAPTER 3

WHAT TYPE OF PROFESSIONAL ARE YOU?: LEARNING FROM YOUR ON-THE-JOB BEHAVIOR

As we reproduce the *familiar*, we assume certain proto-typical roles in the workplace. These roles or types represent common behavioral patterns, and we're going to focus on the following four here:

1. The Fixer
2. The Bully
3. The Avoider
4. The Schmoozer

These are not the only types, but they're ones that we see all the time. They result in behaviors that hold people back in their jobs and careers. By examining these types, we can clearly see how the *familiar* unleashes self-destructive behaviors. We can also learn how to use these behaviors as starting points to drill down, identify, and confront our core issues.

THE RELATIVITY OF ROLES

As soon as you read the list of behavioral types, a mental picture of each probably formed in your mind. To a certain extent, that picture is accurate. Bullies are often hostile, overly demanding tyrants. At the same time, however, bullies can also be amazingly compassionate, caring people. I've worked with a CEO who can be brutal in meetings. Yet people who work for him also have noted that he can be extremely generous and even cry when he talks about how much he values his people. "Which one is real?" they ask. Both of them are.

Keep in mind that these types overlap. Most of you are a mixture of different behavioral traits, which not only include these types but others as well. Some of you are very strong in one of these traits, especially in certain situations—for instance, you're bullies when a subordinate brings you bad news. You need to identify the strong traits that get you in trouble and keep you stuck. Once you identify them, you can find the familiar feelings that produced them and the childhood fears that gave rise to these *familiars*.

The linkage between a childhood fear of being abandoned or not getting your needs met and being an avoider may seem tenuous at first. But as you take a close look at the four types, the connection will become clear.

The Fixer

Just about every organization has fixers. Sometimes they're called "troubleshooters." They're often known as "people persons." Typically, they receive mandates to try to change people with whom no one else has had much success. They're given assignments from bosses along the lines of: "No one has been able to work with John, but I'm sure you can. You're so good with people, I really think you can get somewhere with him." It's likely that these people often fulfill the same role in their personal lives, trying to "fix" a difficult spouse.

Fixers become stuck in their roles. Though they might receive praise from their employers for tackling tough assignments, they often don't advance—they're too valuable as fixers to be promoted. It's also possible that they believe that fixing people is all they can do.

For fixers, the *familiar* is working on lost causes and feeling like they tried their best but still couldn't do much good. As you might suspect, fixers are very dissatisfied with their personal and professional lives. No amount of praise from bosses can stop them from feeling like they're beating their heads against the wall.

Carol is employed by one of the country's leading high-tech companies, and they've literally (though obviously not intentionally) created a job around her *familiar*. An executive vice president sends her around the world to their various offices to work with highly problematic general managers. Typically, these general managers have advanced through the ranks because of their technical proficiency. As managers of employees, however, they're abysmal failures, and they've been promoted to positions where they need to develop some people skills.

Carol, who is based in human resources, may spend a year or two working with each of these individuals. Certainly Carol recognizes that she's talented at helping people deal with their problems, but she's also frustrated that she hasn't advanced much in her company or her career. Sometimes she thinks that she must be doing something wrong. Other times, she feels like a victim and blames the organization for not rewarding her for her efforts.

Recently Carol was telling me about her latest reclamation project, a general manager who constantly distorts communication with his people and won't deal with important issues. After some discussion about the issue,

Carol concluded that now she knows she has to confront him about his flaws. I told her that she was confronting the wrong person. Carol asked me what I meant. I asked her why she wasn't confronting the executive vice president who was sending her out on all these hopeless missions. I suggested that she might ask her boss why he wasn't holding his general managers accountable for growing and developing. This executive was off the hook as long as she was doing his job.

Though Carol was stunned by this new perspective, she eventually got it. But when she got it, the fear that drives her *familiar* immediately surfaced. What if she bowed out of her fixer role? What does she do if she's not traveling around and fixing general managers? The real question is how would she *feel*, and the answer is that she would feel abandoned. If Carol doesn't analyze the source of that feeling of abandonment, she'll remain stuck as a fixer.

Fixers like Carol typically move from one reclamation project to the next, feeling unfulfilled and ungratified. Inside they're thinking: "If I just figure out the right thing to do or say, then . . ." But the "then" is never articulated. Rather, it's the vague hope that if they can just figure things out, they'll finally make that career breakthrough or get that promotion they've always wanted. For many fixers, the solution seems right around the corner, and that illusion keeps them doing the same things they've always done. The payoff for them is simple: *I tried my hardest, I'm not being recognized, and that's the best I can hope for.*

Fixers played this same role in their families. For instance, children who become fixers excelled at everything. They were classic overachievers, straight-A students, excellent athletes, and drama stars. The "fixing" enters into this overachieving because they figure (unconsciously, of course), "If Dad isn't good at what he does, I'll make up for it by being supergood at what I do." They feel that others will assume that Dad isn't so bad after all, because if his kid has done so well, he must have done something right. As a high achiever, the child keeps the focus off Dad and on himself. In his mind, this fixes things.

This role is not the result of growing up in a pathological family; it's simply a normal family that put demands on kids that they couldn't meet. Though the *familiar* still exerts its power when these kids become adults, there's one big difference: Adults have a choice; they can choose not to fix the unfixable. Kids don't have this choice. They've been put in the role of trying to fix Dad and can't afford to realize that the role is inappropriate and impossible to fulfill successfully. Their acceptance into the family system is tied to playing this role.

Common variations on the fixer type include peacemakers and scapegoats. Peacemakers can be quickly identified as people who, when meetings become tense, attempt to provide relief by distracting people from the issue at hand. For example, they're the kind of individuals who, in the middle of a tense discussion, asks anyone if they need coffee. They're trying to fix people who are angry or confronting each other by steering them toward neutral ground. Peacemakers also tend to take the role of team mediators by interrupting arguments and saying, "You really should try to understand his point of view; there's no need to get angry." They're trying to deflect discomfort by making a plea for empty consensus.

Scapegoats fix things in a "negative" way. For instance, a CEO asks a team to report to him on their progress on an important project. The team knows they're never going to meet their target date and fully expect the CEO to tear into them for their failure. During the meeting, one member of the team says, "You know, we wouldn't be so far behind if the marketing people had given us the information when they said they would." This attempt to shift accountability is the last thing the CEO wants to hear, and he focuses his ire on the excuse maker. The team is spared, and the scapegoat is skewered. The scapegoat knows the CEO well enough that he realizes the last thing the guy wants to hear is a weak excuse. Yet the pull of the *familiar* is so strong that he can't help himself. As a child, he was always the one who was picked on at school or was constantly blamed for causing trouble when a group of kids were misbehaving.

Scapegoats like this one may be very bright and likable, but they never go anywhere in their careers because they're always offering excuses about why they (or their team, or their people) didn't deliver. Consciously, they feel like victims, and the current environment reinforces this feeling. Business magazines are filled with stories about "ruthless" CEOs reengineering companies and downsizing workforces. It's easy for scapegoats to feel like victims and blame the environment for their failure to fix things. They don't see that the environment—no matter how tough and demanding—just gives them an excuse to reproduce their *familiar*. Scapegoats are often tremendously self-righteous: "I worked seventy-hour weeks, went all over the world for the company, and when I try to explain why I couldn't achieve the business goal despite all my hard work, my boss doesn't care." That's the payoff. It's not surprising that many scapegoats end up being fired because then they can feel supremely self-righteous: "I gave my organization the best years of my life and now look what they've done to me." It's that old familiar feeling of "no matter how hard I try, no one appreciates me."

The Avoider

Avoiders have great difficulty making the "tough calls" because of the amount of pain these issues raise. Even though they're intellectually aware that someone has let them down or screwed up, they can't confront this person. Instead, they develop rationales and excuses for why this person failed to deliver what was promised. Unable to tolerate the hurt of being disappointed, they protect those people who let them down, avoiding the emotional acknowledgment of what has happened. For them, this feeling of being let down and disappointed is what's familiar.

At the same time, avoiders often believe themselves to be responsible for everyone else's happiness. They can't tolerate hurting someone's feelings or saying no. Parents who are unable to say no to their children are classic avoiders. So too are many owners of small entrepreneurial businesses. They're the ones who never quite make it, and their failures usually have nothing to do with the marketplace. These small business owners avoid confronting the people—customers, suppliers, and employees—who are causing them to lose money and productivity. The irony is that these same business owners may be great at taking financial risks; they're willing to mortgage the house to the hilt to bankroll their restaurant or clothing store. But when it comes to taking the risk required to confront an obnoxious waiter or lazy clerk, they avoid it at all costs—even if it costs them their business. Avoiders find it too painful to tell people that there's something wrong with them. Most often, it goes back to growing up in a family where obvious problems were treated like state secrets. Aunt Hattie smelled bad, Uncle Herman was an addictive gambler, and cousin Ralphie couldn't conduct a coherent conversation with a ferret. But every time avoiders pointed out the obvious, they were made to feel badly about themselves.

Avoiders routinely sabotage themselves. Their attitudes and behaviors are clearly not in their best interests, yet they cling to them with irrational fervor. I used to go to a local dry cleaner who had the rudest, most obnoxious employee I'd ever encountered. The first time she was nasty, I gave her the benefit of the doubt and assumed she'd been having a bad day. But when this behavior repeated itself each and every time I went to the dry cleaner, I spoke to the owner about it. I told him that unless he deals with her and gets her to act like a civilized human being, I would take my business elsewhere. He assured me that he would talk to her and there would be no more problems. The next time I returned, however, she was as mean-spirited as ever. The owner shrugged helplessly when I asked him why he was allowing her to treat customers in this way. Not too many months later, the dry cleaner went out of business.

For avoiders, there's always great pain around the truth. Deep down they believe that if they tell someone the truth—if this dry-cleaning store owner were to tell his clerk to stop being nasty to customers—they'll lose them. They feel they don't deserve anyone better, so they might as well learn to live with the person. Growing up, their parents never listened to them or met their needs, so they feel as if they still don't deserve having employees meet their needs.

If you want to identify a classic avoider, just find a top executive or business owner who says, "We treat our people like family." That's their excuse for never confronting someone who continually messes up and never firing people who do great harm to their teams, departments, or businesses. Many of the individuals who treat their people like family had problematic people in their real families who were never confronted and they worked hard to reproduce that dysfunction in their businesses.

The Bully

Bullies beat people up, and this behavior is so easy to identify that we often oversimplify and misdiagnose the bully's condition. Typically, we assume that bullies were raised by autocratic, authoritarian fathers who substituted barking orders at their kids for a real sense of emotional connectedness, and as a result created younger versions of themselves.

Sometimes this scenario is accurate. Most often, however, bullies are created by giving children everything they want. Affluent families who indulge their children's every whim abandon their kids as surely as parents who literally leave them and don't return. Indulgence substitutes for a real emotional connection. Children intuitively understand that all the gifts, fancy vacations, and other "things" simply mask the fact that the parents really aren't there. There's a television commercial that illustrates this point. A businessman father is driving his son to school when the car breaks down. The father takes out his cell phone, calls for a tow truck, and is informed that it will be at least two hours before one arrives. While they're waiting, the dad asks his kid what he's missing in school, the dad starts telling him what he does, talks about his work, and shows how he can receive a fax. When the tow truck finally pulls up, the kid—who obviously has been having a great time—says that "we're not ready to go yet."

Affluent, indulgent families spend a great deal of time taking their children from point A to point B, but never pause long enough to share meaningful feelings; unless fate intervenes and they break down in their point-A-to-point-B journeys, they never connect in a meaningful way. This is especially a problem for men, who are encouraged and rewarded for doing rather than being. Only when we stop focusing on being the "cruise director" and the entertainment coordinator can we truly engage in a relationship with our children. Emotional openness and vulnerability, not the nature or frequency of the activity, is the foundation for meaningful involvement with a child.

Abandonment is central to the bully's *familiar*. Feeling abandoned, disappointed, and isolated are the feelings that bullies reproduce in the workplace through their intimidation and temper tantrums. We've worked with a number of bullies, and when we've asked them if they know how poorly they treat people, they respond something like this: "I get so frustrated, they never do it right no matter how many times I tell them what I need. Just once I wish someone would anticipate my needs instead of making me go over and over the same thing. I'm disappointed, and that's why I yell at them."

Of course they're disappointed. Bullies have an uncanny ability to surround themselves with people who are guaranteed to come up short and frustrate them. Or they set their expectations so high that no one will ever meet them. As a result, they start screaming and pushing people around, and many of those people end up quitting. That puts them right back at their *familiar*: abandonment. Sometimes the bully's actions don't cause people to quit but make any real emotional connection impossible; their intimidating tactics keep people at a distance, and this reproduces the familiar feeling of isolation, even though they may be surrounded by people.

It's instructive to note that a good way of dealing with a bully is to punch him in the nose. Not literally, of course, but figuratively. When a kid stands up to the playground bully and bops him on the snout, it sends a clear message that he's not going to tolerate him acting that way. Similarly, we need to challenge bullies by saying, "What's going on? Why are you acting like a maniac?"

Such questions might anger them initially, but ultimately it will help them examine their core issues. Most people don't realize that anger is a secondary emotion. That initial rage response covers a great deal of hurt and a sense of loss. Challenging that rage often allows bullies to focus on deeper issues. A challenge, however, is very different from a provocation. Bullies are provoked by excuses and by passive-aggressive behavior. If you say to a bully, "You've got a lot of nerve screaming about working overtime on the project when you've been on vacation for the last two weeks; we've all got other obligations besides work, you know," you'll either provoke him or end up in a power struggle that he's certain to win and you're sure to lose. A challenge is listening to an irrational tirade and responding: "Why are you so worked up about this? I've heard you make that point before. What else is going on?"

Bullies need to be attuned to the intensity of their responses; they need to catch themselves responding in ways that are out of proportion to the reality of situations. The bullying CEO we've referred to earlier now is aware of what triggers his brutalizing behaviors. When someone says or does something that formerly would trigger an explosion, the CEO is now able to process it and head off a tirade. Because he's aware of his issues and has a sense of from where they come, he can often receive disappointing news without flying off the handle. He recognizes that as disappointing as that news is, it's nothing compared to his father throwing him out of the house, or, just as bad, ignoring him by indulging him.

At the same time, however, bullies are often returned to their *familiar* by the people around them. As much as this CEO wants to grow and develop and reach the next level, some of the people around him need him to return to his old role. There's one sales executive in particular who interacts with the CEO as if he's following a script. Typically, the CEO will say something positive like, "Things really seem to be going well," and this executive will respond, "Well, not in Topeka." The problem may be minor; the issues may be easily resolved. But the CEO automatically begins obsessing about Topeka; he starts screaming over the phone at people in his Topeka office; he engages in lengthy diatribes with the executive who raised the issue about how the Topeka people need to get their act together.

It should come as no surprise that this sales executive grew up in a family where making Dad upset was the norm. When his CEO isn't upset, he feels lost. Better the CEO he knows, no matter how much he shouts and belittles, than the CEO he doesn't know. When the CEO becomes upset, this sales executive knows himself exactly.

The Schmoozer

Schmoozers create the illusion of relationships. They know lots of people but never establish meaningful relationships because they don't take risks. Specifically, they don't risk intimacy and vulnerability. They prefer keeping relationships on a superficial level and thus avoid the risk of being hurt.

No matter what is going on in a schmoozer's life—no matter how many awful things have happened to him—he'll always tell you that things are going great. Even if everyone knows something bad has happened, the schmoozer is great at rationalizing and minimizing it, saying things like, "Well, it's all for the best." To admit that something terrible has happened or that he's disappointed or depressed is tremendously difficult for a schmoozer. To him it's not just saying that things are bad now, but that things will be bad forever.

Typically, schmoozers grew up with at least one depressed person. Mom or Dad sulked around the house, casting a pall over everyone and everything. When schmoozers admit that everything isn't great, they're right back with that depressed person who wouldn't let them have a moment of happiness. To share a deeply felt anxiety with a colleague would be a major risk, and would invite a painful intrusion. The schmoozer's *familiar* is to feel like a long-suffering victim, and by pretending to be on top of the world and creating superficial relationships, schmoozers are right back at that *familiar*.

To understand how this is so, let's look at two examples of schmoozers.

Chet is a computer company sales executive who has coasted for years. His schmoozing, industry contacts, and product knowledge have not only kept him employed but earned him occasional bonuses and promotions. A few years ago, though, things changed. Under intense pressure due to falling margins and overseas competition, Chet's company downsized and restructured. A new CEO was brought in, and he clearly communicated that these organizational changes were just the beginning.

Not surprisingly, Chet feared for his job. He'd barely escaped the first downsizing, and he suspected he wouldn't escape the next one. The moderate results that had kept him safe in the past no longer sufficed; Chet was being asked to improve his performance, and despite his best efforts, he seemed unable to do so.

One day in a sales meeting, Chet tried to explain to his boss how he was supposed to close a sale the previous day but failed to do so. "I just couldn't get an appointment with the guy I needed to see," Chet said. His boss castigated him. He was chewed out because he had promised that he would have a response from his customer by the time of the meeting. His boss lectured Chet about accountability and gave him a handout titled "Ten Keys to Closing a Sale."

Chet left the meeting with the demeanor of a whipped dog, promising to "do better." Of course, he won't do better until he becomes aware of the familiar feeling he's reproducing. After much discussion, Chet saw the similarity between his performance at the sales meeting and how he felt when he played football in high school. Back then, no matter how well he played, his father always found a shortcoming in his performance and embarrassed him publicly by pointing it out. Like many schmoozers, Chet placed himself in situations and did things that brought him severe criticism that made him feel like a victim. If Chet had a real, meaningful relationship with his customer, none of this would ever have happened.

Schmoozing behavior, however, can take other forms. Schmoozers are not always prototypical salespeople with a fake smile and an empty line of patter. For instance, an administrative assistant named Carla who worked for a major company fit the type, though she wasn't the back-slapping, garrulous sort. Instead, she was the type of person who would do anything her superiors asked her to do. When asked if she could work late on a project, she would say, "Sure, don't worry, my family understands." If she were asked to do additional work not covered by her job description, she'd tell managers that she was glad to do it because the assignment was new and challenging.

One day Carla told her superiors that she was unhappy and wanted to quit. She complained that she was underpaid, that her family resented her late hours, and that the company was asking her to do things that she wasn't originally hired to do. Her desire to quit came as a shock to many people in the company. For years she'd proclaimed everything was fine and worked without complaint, and now she had a laundry list of problems. Her schmoozer's superficial relationships prevented any of her coworkers from getting close enough to see how upset she was. As a schmoozer Carla was content to suffer in silence, feeling victimized and alone.

Test Yourself: What Type Are You?

The following quiz is designed to help you identify the type of behavior you most commonly exhibit. For each type, I've created a list of questions. Add up your "yes" responses for each type. The one with the most is your type (in reality, of course, you're a mixture of different types—this is merely the one that is dominant).

After you identify your type, don't stop there. Drilling down to the feelings and past experiences that produced this behavior is essential; knowing your type is simply an important first step.

Fixer

1. Do you have a reputation as a troubleshooter in your organization?
2. Are you considered a people person by others; someone who can really handle difficult employees?
3. Are you often given assignments to coach, mentor, and confront people who are causing problems?
4. Do you feel like the patron saint of lost causes?
5. Do you believe that as hard as you try, you're not being recognized for your hard work or rewarded with promotions, salary increases, etc.?
6. Growing up, were you a high achiever?
7. Do you recall trying to fix things in your family as a child, trying to make up for something someone else was unable to do or achieve?
8. When things become tense in meetings, do you attempt to calm everyone down or break the tension in some way?
9. Do you find yourself (consciously or not) taking the blame when things go wrong?
10. Do you feel like a victim?

Avoider

1. Do you have difficulty confronting people?
2. Instead of confronting, do you automatically come up with a rationale or excuse for why someone messed up or let you down?
3. Do you believe you protect people who let you down?

4. Do you find it difficult to say no?
5. Will you do just about anything to avoid hurting someone's feelings?
6. Have there been instances when you didn't deal with subordinates even though they were unproductive, unprofessional in their conduct, or costing you (or your organization) money?
7. Did you grow up in a family where family members' flaws (a drinking problem, emotional instability, laziness) were never discussed?
8. As a child, if you pointed out these flaws, did the family make you feel badly for doing so?
9. Do you fear that if you confront someone with the truth, they won't be able to handle it?
10. Have you ever said, "We treat our people like family"?

Bully

1. Do you frequently lose your temper at work and intimidate people?
2. Do you find that your tendency to explode keeps people at a distance?
3. Do you feel justified in becoming furious because you believe people let you down?
4. When people make excuses, do you fly off the handle?
5. When you berate and belittle people, have you ever said (or thought) anything like, "I wish someone here would anticipate my needs for a change rather than make me say things again and again"?

6. Are you surrounded by people who seem to have an uncanny knack for disappointing and frustrating you?
7. Did you grow up in a home ruled by an autocratic, authoritarian parent?
8. Did you grow up in an affluent household where you were indulged and even spoiled?
9. Was it rare for your parents to share meaningful feelings with you?
10. After you explode at someone in your workplace, do you feel regretful and abandoned?

Schmoozer

1. Do you know lots of people but possess few, if any, meaningful relationships?
2. To avoid being hurt, do you prefer to keep most of your relationships "casual"?
3. When people ask you how things are going, are you likely to respond, "Great!"?
4. Do you tend to rationalize and minimize negative events?
5. Is it difficult for you to admit that you're disappointed or depressed?
6. Did you grow up with at least one parent who was often depressed, who moped around and accomplished little?
7. Looking back on your childhood, did someone make it difficult for you to experience sustained happiness or pleasure?
8. Even though you're angry or upset about the way you're being treated, do you pretend that everything is fine?

9. Do you routinely place yourself in situations where you receive criticism?
10. Do you secretly believe not only that things are bad for you now, but that they'll be bad forever?

WE'VE ALL BEEN TYPECAST TO A CERTAIN EXTENT

When contemplating your responses to these questions and how they relate to your feelings while growing up, don't think for a second that you're unusual. All of us have fallen into certain types of behavioral patterns because of how we were raised. No family is perfect. Every family burdens their children with realistic fears—of not getting their needs met, of being abandoned—around which they create familiar feelings as adults. There are many bullies, fixers, avoiders, schmoozers, and other types out there, and the difference between us is a matter of degree and the mixture of types.

You can't escape the confining nature of your type unless you're willing to explore your internal frontier. People like Chet and Carla don't have a clue about what's happening to them emotionally. While their behaviors are often predictable, their real emotions are masked from both outsiders and themselves. They haven't done the internal work necessary to achieve emotional consistency.

Great leaders are distinguished by their emotional consistency or congruency. They always communicate their feelings clearly; they're in touch with how they feel and why they're feeling that way. The people who work for them and with them greatly appreciate this consistency, knowing that they won't get a reaction out of left field.

This emotional consistency is especially important in a Fifth Wave world where everything else is wildly unpredictable. Markets are constantly surprising us, jobs are changing rapidly or even ceasing to exist, and technology is advancing at such a rapid rate that today's innovation is tomorrow's anachronism. Given all this, we gravitate toward leaders who possess an emotional core that doesn't vary.

At the same time, emotional consistency gives leaders—and all of us—a sense of security that we can no longer get from external sources. When you don't have that consistency, you're uncertain about your feelings; you respond a certain way and wonder, "Where did that come from?" Confused and confounded by your emotions and by the types of behaviors they spawn, you become indecisive and fearful.

No matter what your type might be, the way out of its negative effects is exploring the territory inside you and developing the emotional consistency that comes with a healthy *familiar*.

CHAPTER 4

THE BLOCKERS THAT HOLD YOU BACK

Why is it so difficult to leave our old, unhealthy *familiars* behind and create new *familiars*? Why can't we simply recognize that what we're doing is harming our careers or work effectiveness, and change our behaviors?

Because powerful "blockers" keep us stuck in the same old place and prevent us from trying anything new. Even if we recognize intellectually that our behaviors are counterproductive, blockers distort and repack information to fit our *familiars*. We can't translate our intellectual recognition into appropriate action because old feelings get in the way. For instance, I regularly work with managers to teach them how to hold others accountable. Intellectually, they understand the process. Emotionally, however, they often distort what we've taught them. For some of them, accountability somehow translates into verbally brutalizing subordinates. They immediately escalate their displeasure with a missed deadline into an intimidating ultimatum: "If you don't deliver the next project on time, you're out of here!" When I confront them with their actions, they look bewildered and say, "That's what you taught me to do; I'm just holding them accountable."

When most people talk about what's blocking them in their professional lives, they usually refer to things such as a lack of education, the need to find a new employer, problems with crazy bosses, and the like. As we'll see later in the chapter, these are false blockers.

The real blockers that impact most people are *contrast places* and *symbols*. They block people at a deep, internal level. If you don't drill down, you probably will never unearth these blockers. The other blocker that I'll discuss is a *position power model*, and it obstructs your ability to grow and change in a more external way; it sets up situations that discourage self-discovery and encourage power struggles, gamesmanship, and other stagnating behaviors.

CONTRAST PLACES: THE PARADOX OF DOING GOOD AND FEELING BAD

At some point in your life, you've probably done something well or achieved a goal yet felt inexplicably sad, irritated, or upset. This disconcerting paradox is a result of a **contrast place.** You're in a contrast place when you receive a positive payoff for behavior in the present that you received a negative payoff for in the past. In other words, you're valued in the here and now for being someone who was devalued and depreciated in the past.

A contrast place can be tricky to understand. Sometimes people simplify the concept to being rewarded in the present for something you were punished for in the past. This simple definition makes a contrast place more about actions than feelings. The feeling state is crucial to understanding the concept, as the following example demonstrates.

A number of years ago I worked with members of a large medical practice to help them build better relationships both within the practice and with their patients. Communication had almost completely broken down among the staff, and feedback from patients was increasingly negative. One doctor in particular exemplified the practice's (and perhaps the profession's) dilemma and illustrated the power of a contrast place. He had put in a great deal of effort to help one of his patients rehabilitate from a stroke. Working hard on the patient's behalf, he directed the therapies that resulted in the patient's relatively fast recovery. The patient and his family showered the doctor with praise, telling him what a great physician and human being he was. After feeling touched initially and pleased by this praise, the doctor began feeling down and out of sorts. Unconsciously, this praise brought him back to when he was a child and would try to please his parents by cleaning up his room or taking out the garbage, but they would say things like, "If you really cared about me, you'd be a good boy all the time and not just when you felt like it."

If his patients recognize that he has significantly changed their lives, why didn't his parents allow him to have an impact on their lives? When we're young, a major drive is to impact key people in our lives. When we're robbed of that impact, we begin to doubt ourselves.

As a young boy, the doctor's parents didn't allow him to have this impact. As a result the contrast, between what he felt as a boy and what he feels as a man, hurts. The doctor naturally doesn't want to feel this pain again, so he does everything possible to avoid receiving demonstrative praise from patients. As a result of this blocker, the doctor is right back at his *familiar:* feeling that no matter what he does, he doesn't get validated for it. Rather than showing his feelings and involvement in his work and having patients love and praise him, the doctor ends up with an emotionally empty encounter and avoids effusive compliments.

This doctor isn't unique. Many health-care professionals depersonalize relationships with patients to avoid a contrast place. By doing so, they harm the effectiveness of their diagnosis and treatment. When there's no real relationship between patient and doctor, communication is hampered; patients are afraid to ask questions and doctors don't level with patients.

I see this sort of self-sabotaging behavior all the time in people with whom I work. As much as some of them want to be successful and effective, they're blocked by their contrast places. A CEO recognizes that his over-reactions and verbal tongue-lashings of people are counterproductive behaviors. At the same time, however, his contrast place frequently blocks him from changing his behaviors. When he was successful in his family as a child, he was severely critized for what he didn't do. Now, as an incredibly successful CEO, he often receives kudos for his achievements. When this happens, he sometimes reacts by alienating and offending those who compliment him on his success. Better to leave a trail of offended and angry employees in his wake than to face the fact that his parents couldn't appreciate him, but his employees can.

SYMBOLISM

Symbols are emotional clones from our past. They are people in our lives today who elicit the same feelings as people who were important to us growing up. Typically,

CEOs and other strong leaders are symbols for demanding, intrusive parents. My wife's father was often tyrannical, and as a child Arleah coped with his hostility by trying to "disappear." When she encounters a business leader whom she *expects* to respond in a way similar to her father, Arleah's initial response to this symbol is to disappear—to remain silent or make herself scarce. It's a response that Arleah has learned to avoid through methods that we'll discuss.

"Expects" is an important word in understanding symbols, since symbols are about expected responses—responses on the part of both parties. Symbols become blockers when we give them the same power over our lives that the person from the past wielded. We get caught up in symbols because the current behavior of the symbolic person produces enough familiar feelings to build an emotional bridge from the present to the past.

We often respond to symbols in ways that have little to do with their current impact and everything to do with our history. When trying to identify a symbol, it's often a mistake to focus on how people look or even how they act. It's the similar feelings that are crucial. We've worked with a young executive whose goals have been set unrealistically high, and she needs to talk to her boss about resetting her goals. This executive, however, struggled to ask her boss to do this because her boss is a symbol for her father. If she were to ask her father the same question, he would have responded, "You contracted for these goals. Do it! No more discussion!"

Her boss, who was a woman, could be rigid and demanding at times. That's why her boss's expected response recalled her father's typical reaction. The symbol's power was such that she expected to feel as diminished and worthless as she felt as a child.

Symbols block us with these expected responses. What we expect often has nothing to do with reality, but it has the power to prevent us from making a reasonable request or taking other actions that would help us be more productive. A supervisor might have snapped at us only once in five years, but that one time was enough to trigger our memory of someone who humiliated us growing up. Even though this supervisor is usually even-tempered, we dread dealing with him, not because of who he is but because he's become a symbol.

THE POSITION POWER MODEL

The model that governs many workplace relationships makes it very difficult for people to do Internal Frontier work; this model blocks self-discovery because it creates an environment that rewards manipulative behaviors and allows feelings to stay hidden. The position power model holds that people get things done because they're ordered to do them. It sets up a system based on power struggles where there are winners and losers; it builds up distrust between people who work together, especially people who occupy different positions of power. Typically, an employee carries out an order from a boss believing that it can't possibly work to his benefit; he is suspicious about the manager's motives; he does what he is told to do, but he doesn't bring much enthusiasm or creativity to the task. This type of relationship works against change and growth. It blocks people from engaging in relationships that foster the openness and vulnerability that allow people to address core issues and feelings.

We've worked with one executive who is genuinely kind and gentle and believes in our approach, but he is also firmly entrenched in the position power model.

PRODUCTIVITY IS AFFECTED BY:	
The Influence Model	**The Position Power Model**
Requires:	Requires:
High Trust/Delegation	Constant Monitoring
Relationships	Transactions
Conflict Resolution	Orders
And results in:	And results in:
Freed Energy	Contained Energy
Growth of Work Force	Perpetual Power Struggles
Security is:	Security is:
Value-Based	Transient
Internal	External

The Shechtman Institute
Fifth Wave Leadership ™

When you call him on the phone, he answers by barking out his last name like a warning. He acts like a drill sergeant with his people, routinely berating and belittling subordinates when they make mistakes. This executive doesn't trust himself enough to stop bossing people around. The position power model encourages him to stay stuck in this low-trust posture, avoiding taking the risk of being open with people and possibly being hurt by them.

THE INFLUENCE MODEL

The influence model is an alternative approach that facilitates the openness, trust, and vulnerability critical to relationship-building and blocker-breaking. It encourages the internal exploration necessary for growth and development. Bob Kerrigan at Northwestern Mutual in

Los Angeles has refined this model and implemented it with great success in his organization. As the name suggests, influence models don't *force* people to do things. Instead, they create an environment where people *want* to do things. In an influence model, the culture of the organization, not raw power, is the change agent. Clearly articulated values coupled with consistent and congruent behaviors create an environment that is persuasive and compelling. By communicating openly and honestly, people respond to others as part of a real relationship. Each holds the other accountable. Influence models produce emotionally honest relationships where individuals express and explore their feelings rather than deny them (to themselves and others).

In the position power model, transactions take precedence over relationships. As a result, people don't have the chance to deal with their issues in a relationship and consequently are blocked in their growth. You can't form a productive relationship with people who don't trust themselves or you. You need that trust to foster open, honest, and direct communication that can change someone's perspective and behaviors. Time after time, we see the pattern of managers giving orders and employees responding with malicious compliance.

Influence models give people choices, encourage risk-taking and facilitate trust. The goal is to create an emotionally healthy environment where unhealthy *familiars* can be addressed.

FALSE BLOCKERS

When we talk about being blocked in our careers or in our work performance, we often identify superficial obstacles. Rather than face the fact that blockers such as contrast places and symbols are inside of us, we set up convenient excuses for our failures. Here are some common examples of false blockers:

Not having the right degree or type of education. "I need an MBA to get ahead in this company (or industry)" is a common complaint. But in this culture, it's largely an empty one. Many of the most successful, entrepreneurial companies are headed by people without advanced degrees. Some of the most successful people in the high-tech industry dropped out of college to start their businesses. This false blocker only acquires power when you confuse core skills with job knowledge. My ability to build relationships and make decisions is far more valuable in a fast-moving global economy than my training in cost accounting or marketing. We get our priorities mixed up, and put false blockers in place, because of higher education's emphasis on knowing about everything but ourselves, on exploring external frontiers and ignoring internal ones.

Missing the right skills or training. Training mania has people in its grip. Seminars, workshops, and executive-development programs offer the false promise of providing people with "magical" bits of information. Many ambitious professionals sincerely believe that a guru or a training program can provide them with data or competencies that will unblock them. People tell them: "You should really attend that six-week leadership program, then you'll position yourself for a promotion." This is nonsense. Information addicts, however, have convinced themselves that the way to break through to the next level is through external means.

Not meeting the right people (or being in the wrong place at the wrong time). We're awash in networkers who jump from one business social function to another, attempting to make connections. Instead of building relationships, they're just schmoozing, and that will get them nowhere. Still, they're convinced they're not getting anywhere because they don't know the right people. Or they blame their organizations for not training them properly or giving them challenging assignments. Or they believe their boss is a jerk and is holding them back. The real problem is that they're not forming productive relationships with the people they do know.

These false blockers are attractive because there's a bit of truth in all of them. On average, people who graduate from highly rated law schools have a greater chance of initial success than many other lawyers; it's important to have specific skills and knowledge in order to perform competently; and it makes perfect sense to know people who can help you in your career. But in a Fifth Wave world, these things are far less important than in the past. Lacking any of them won't leave a black mark on your record. On the other hand, if you're a skilled Harvard lawyer who networks to beat the band but has never dealt with your core issues and blockers, your road to success can be slow, tortuous, and unsatisfying.

REAL BLOCKERS ARE INSIDIOUS IN THEIR EFFECT

Never underestimate the damage blockers can do or the "invisible" ways in which they do their damage. When you're facing a significant challenge in your professional life and really need to break from your old *familiar* to change and grow, blockers emerge. As self-aware as my wife Arleah is, she still is bedeviled by contrast places and symbols.

A year or two ago, we were doing consulting work for a client and Arleah was having a great deal of trouble focusing in our meetings. She told me she felt "bumbling and inept," and her behavior reflected these feelings— she had trouble articulating her thoughts and sometimes had a lost look on her face.

Our main client contact was a clear symbol for her father; his fierce, bullying demeanor made her feel as small and unimportant as her father did. Similarly, Arleah would make a suggestion in the meeting that was hailed as insightful and tremendously valuable, and she'd feel awful. The contrast place was produced by the accolades she was receiving now, contrasted with how her suggestions had been derided or dismissed in the past.

Blocked, Arleah would resort to the behavior she had used successfully as a child. She would look so lost and uncomfortable that someone invariably would come to her rescue. By assuming a pained, confused expression, she could provoke her parents to ask what was wrong and be given rare permission to speak directly about what was troubling her. The fuzziness in Arleah's head emerged as inarticulate verbal responses and a pained, confused expression. At first, she was confounded by her lack of clarity and directness in these meetings. Over time, however, she came to understand where and how she was being blocked and was able to minimize the impact of her symbol and contrast place.

Blockers can stymie anyone. The first step is awareness of their existence. The second step is clearing them out of the way with some essential tools of the Internal Frontier process—tools you'll discover in the next chapter.

THE PROCESS

A MAP TO EXPLORE THE INTERNAL FRONTIER

CHAPTER 5

START OUT BY RECOGNIZING AND REMOVING YOUR BLOCKERS

In real life, the Internal Frontier process can be launched in a number of ways. Sometimes it begins within the confines of an accountability group or when I'm called in by an organization to work with a given individual. Sometimes people begin this self-discovery process by entering into a reciprocal, growth-focused relationship where feelings are expressed and explored. Others begin the process on their own and in an intuitive fashion, confronting a personal issue that has been causing them great difficulty and translating that confrontation into professional growth.

I'll talk about these pathways in ensuing chapters. Here we'll start with the process of removing blockers, partly because contrast places and symbols are still fresh in your mind and partly because they're good to deal with at the beginning, so that they don't ambush you later on.

A CONTINGENCY PLAN FOR CONTRAST PLACES

One of the best ways of blasting through blockers is to ask the following question: *Is there anything in the present reality that warrants me feeling this badly?*

Recognizing that there's a disconnect between the way you feel and the reality of the situation is a great first step. Being aware of a discrepancy between feelings and realities gives us the chance to think before reacting. Let me share with you how this helps me. While I enjoy the recognition that comes with public speaking and being interviewed by the media, I also am aware that the initial feeling of satisfaction and happiness is often followed by sadness and irritability. Shortly thereafter I become extremely picky and overreact when something falls short of my expectations. Since I spend so much of my time on planes, flight attendants often bear the brunt of my irritation after I've given a speech or an article appears.

When I question whether there's anything in current reality that justifies my feeling so irritable and angry, I realize that a contrast place has impacted my behavior. This is especially true when the reaction from an audience has been overwhelmingly positive (of course, when I perform poorly, I have a good reason to feel irritable and angry).

I grew up in a large, extended family who argued about anything and everything that came up in conversation. Many of my relatives were convinced that their primary role in life was to give the upcoming generation a hard time. Some did this out of their own personal unhappiness, some out of a perverse belief that this was good training for the entrepreneurs they hoped their young relatives would become. When told my ideas weren't quite right and that I harbored odd notions, I responded by defending virtually every observation I made and every experience I had. I was denied the opportunity to connect with people who were important in my life and to know that what I believed made a difference.

After I speak and I'm greeted with resounding applause and people telling me how much my talk meant to them, I'm deeply touched and gratified. Then I'm deeply saddened. Why couldn't my family recognize what my audiences and the media are recognizing: that my ideas are worthwhile? It's sad to think that my family didn't appreciate my perspective, and this feeling can block me from reacting appropriately. This sadness segues to irritation, and then to anger, when I realize how easy it could have been for my extended family to validate some of my perceptions and how it hurt to be continually depreciated. When I find myself wanting to bite the head off a flight attendant, it puts me on alert. It's a red flag that I'm in a contrast place, and that's when I put my emotional contingency plan into action.

As the name implies, an emotional contingency plan gives me an alternative way of reacting when I fall into a contrast place. The message flashes in my head: "Look out, Morrie. Your irritability factor is through the roof; be alert you don't jump on someone for something that isn't his fault." When present reality doesn't jibe with your feelings, you may be in a contrast place, and that's when you need an alternative way of viewing how you're feeling. If you don't have a plan to fall back on, you're likely to behave in a way that causes you and the people around you harm and prevents you from being as effective as you otherwise might be.

DIMINISHING THE POWER OF SYMBOLS

Symbols don't block us as much when we know who they represent. Identifying the person from our past who has given rise to a symbol isn't always easy. We've put defense systems in place that often prevent us from immediately recognizing who that person is. For instance, every workplace has individuals who attempt to please everyone. They're the ones who rarely, if ever, make requests or statements that cause any type of friction in a relationship. This pleasing behavior is a defense against the power of symbols. By pleasing everyone, they don't have to be thrown back to that pivotal person from their past. Another defense is to develop an extraordinary tolerance for inappropriate behaviors. When someone makes sexually crude and offensive comments, Jack responds, "Oh, that's just the way he is, he always acts that way." Jack had deadened his emotional responses, enabling him to avoid dealing with the pain a symbol elicits.

To break through these defenses and identify our symbols, we need to look beyond physical or behavioral traits (because people in our present often look and act differently from those in our past) for a similarity in feelings. We need to ask ourselves what important figures from our past (family members, close family friend, coach, child-care provider, etc.) made us feel the same way as someone we work with.

If you're still stumped about who this person is, ask yourself the following questions:

> *What relationships drain and frustrate me the most at work and at home, and what relationships do they most closely resemble from my past?*

> *Who makes me feel like I can never get anywhere with them? Who are the people with whom I have unresolvable issues (both as an adult and as a child)?*

After we help our clients identify symbolic individuals, we then demonstrate that the person with whom they're currently dealing is not the person in their past. While this fact is intellectually obvious, it's emotionally obscure. By acknowledging this fact—by talking about how a boss isn't your father—you move the blocker off to the side. When we helped the young executive mentioned in the previous chapter recognize this truth, she was able to talk to her boss about resetting her goals. It wasn't easy for her to do. Even though she had a much clearer understanding of her symbol, the emotional leap she took was scary.

People often need to take a risk to reduce the power of a symbol. Typically, they're afraid of confronting a symbolic figure over an issue. They tell us, "I can't do that. If I do, I might lose everything." At worst, what they might lose is their job. What they need to understand is that losing their job is not comparable to the loss of intimacy with their mother or father. As painful as that loss might have been in the past, no one in the present (especially a boss) has that power. The risk they have to take, therefore, is losing the relationship. By being willing to put a relationship on the line— by saying something that you feel will cause your boss to have a negative reaction—you start removing the blocker. It's possible that you could be fired. If you have a boss who is a lunatic, his reaction may well be as radical as you anticipated (and if so, you're probably better off working for someone else). But even then, you'll find that the loss is tolerable, that it's nothing like putting a relationship with a parent at risk. In most instances, however, people discover that they don't lose the relationship and that they emotionally survive the encounter. Instead, their willingness to take that risk creates credibility with the other person, and helps resolve the issue.

THE GRIEVING PROCESS

Grieving is a critical internal frontier process. It helps people identify the key losses in their lives and links their feelings to what really caused them.

A CEO with whom I've worked closely, for example, is very conscious of his overreactions and tirades in response to relatively minor problems. He knows that he should change his behavior. What makes it difficult for him to do so is the profound sadness of what he's lost and how it still dominates his life. He is reminded of the loss that occurred when he was growing up—his parents' inability to meet his needs—when his people disappoint him. Unless he grieves this loss, he will continue to repeat the same unproductive behaviors.

For this CEO, grieving means understanding that this loss is irrevocably part of his past. It's acknowledging that he can never make up for it or exact vengeance for it. There's absolutely nothing he can do in the present to get back what he wished his parents had given him. When he gets blocked, it's because he's trying to make up for something he never had. In one sense, he hopes his people will never disappoint him as his parents did. Even if that were possible, it wouldn't make up for what they were unable to give him emotionally. Grieving this loss—acknowledging it, sitting with it, and feeling it deeply—is the only way to unlock its hold on him.

What I'm talking about is an emotional recognition of intellectual reality—in other words, experiencing the profound sadness of what happened versus knowing what went wrong. Many people I work with assume that because they know what their problem is, they've taken care of it. On a number of occasions, people have told us things like, "Oh, I've been in therapy, I know that my family had no time for me growing up and I was shunted off to the side. I responded to the way they treated me by being a high achiever and learned how to get what I want by doing very well. So I have that one solved."

When I ask these people how all this makes them feel, they usually respond that they've put the whole thing behind them.

The problem here is that they treat a terribly sad loss as if it were a business deal—"I've analyzed the problem and signed off on it." Intellectual recognition of the issue is fine, but all it really does is make you more informed about why you're so neurotic. Grieving involves acknowledging that the sad feelings you have are part of who you are and that you can't dispose of them like a defective piece of equipment.

Many people are unwilling to grieve their losses. It's very difficult—and very frightening—to admit that there are things which happened to us that we can't undo. It's easier to deny that these issues from our past still bother us than to accept and grieve them. The feelings associated with both contrast places and symbols are very powerful, and we shy away from confronting the emotional losses that created them. If they're not grieved, however, we are blocked from growth and fall back on our *familiars*.

When I say that people fail to grieve their losses, I mean that they fail to grieve them properly. Most people shut down their feelings about the losses in their past and simply feel a little bad all the time. This is *chronic grief*, and what we help people do is convert it to *acute grief*. Instead of shutting down our feelings, we encourage people to experience them fully and deal with them so they can move on. When we allow ourselves to experience these feelings, there's a beginning, a middle, and an end. If we shut them down, they solidify and block us.

Acute grief isn't pretty to look at, but it's mercifully brief. One manager in the process of converting his chronic grief to acute grief had been sitting around his office "not acting like himself," or so coworkers commented. It's not that he ceased to care about what went on in the office; it was simply that he was coming to terms with how awful it felt being figuratively abandoned as a child. For a little while, he was distracted as he focused on his feelings. But he gradually came out of it, and when he did he emerged far more functional and focused than before.

Still, experiencing acute grief doesn't magically make the sadness go away. It does, however, cause the grief to come and go in diminishing waves. The wave of grief hits and hurts, but over time it comes less and less often. Between the waves, you can function normally. The key is allowing yourself a bad moment every once in a while. Anyone who believes he has to live up to the old paradigm of a tough business leader who hides his feelings from associates will have trouble granting himself permission to experience a little sadness every now and then.

DON'T TRY THIS ALONE

Acute grief can't simply be experienced in isolation. It must be felt within a relationship. This requires taking a major risk. People need to sit down with someone they trust and begin to speak the unspeakable: "This feels like the worst possible time in my life. I feel terrible about my career and my relationships; there's nothing I feel right about." They need to cry or do whatever is necessary to acknowledge their emotions.

We get unstuck when we bring these feelings into the open and allow another person to see how we feel. Blockers are formidable obstacles when we keep our feelings to ourselves. For instance, an entrepreneur who formed a highly innovative business in the seventies refuses to acknowledge that his great idea is now run-of-the-mill. Until he verbalizes how badly he feels about this, he's going to continue to run the business as if his original idea was still as viable as it was twenty-five years ago. Though intellectually he might recognize that the business has changed, he needs to articulate his feelings about this fact before he can move on to a new, more effective strategy.

A significant number of my clients are middle-aged business executives whose children have left for college, and some of these empty nesters continue to cling to their kids. One very successful entrepreneur has a son who plays college football, and he travels around the country to every single game, refusing to miss a game no matter what other important things are taking place in his life. While it's fine to want to attend his son's games, it's not OK to be driven by an obsessive need to be at every game. It's very sad to realize that our parenting days are over—that our kids no longer need us on a continuous basis—but we need to talk about these sad feelings to someone, or we'll be stuck.

We form relationships with people in order to make the covert overt. Whether it's your spouse, your colleague, or someone else, you need to have at least one person to whom you can express your sadness. The more successful we become, however, the more difficult it is to form this type of relationship with someone we work with or who works for us. CEOs and other leaders tell us that there's no one with whom they can be open or vulnerable.

They're concerned that if they share their grief with anyone, it will be viewed as a sign of weakness. Certainly there's some validity to this concern. It's difficult to assemble a management team, inspire confidence in partners, or build a company from scratch if you confess that you feel miserable and are struggling with key areas of your life. On the other hand, it's even more difficult to do these things if you feel miserable, your life is falling apart, and you keep these feelings locked up inside. You need to exercise some common sense in whom you choose as a relationship partner, but it's a far better alternative than wallowing in chronic grief and letting it block you.

You may also find it difficult to share your grief with another person because you begin to depend on them, and fear losing them or being controlled by them. Given the volatility of the workplace and high turnover rates, it's quite possible that you will lose them. Many executives feel betrayed when a trusted adviser or subordinate leaves to take another job. "Boy, did that guy screw me," they complain. "I trained him, I was his mentor, and this is how he pays me back." Again, it's true that people invest a great deal of time and emotional energy in relationships and are very disappointed when those relationships end. But rather than get stuck in feelings of betrayal, you need to acknowledge how sad you feel about losing this person and then form another equally important relationship. This transition is facilitated when we separate the past from the present.

A HEALTHY SIGN THAT YOU'RE WORKING AT REMOVING BLOCKERS

Beware of those who suffer in silence and pretend to "go along with the program." I'm referring to those people who never cause problems and accept everything without question. On the outside, it may appear that they're doing fine. In many cases, however, they are living lives of quiet desperation. One of the best ways to remove blockers is to create problems in your life.

People create problems because they know something has to change. An executive we've worked with is known to carry my first book around the office with him and use it as a cudgel. He will storm into a subordinate's office, brandish the book, and say, "We don't do things this way around here, look at Chapter 8, page 103 if you don't believe me." He offends people left and right and resists feedback as if it were poison. Intellectually, he understands my point about building relationships, yet he's totally opaque about how he's perceived. He is certainly aware that he should listen to people, but after listening for a few seconds, he tunes them out.

But he tries. He makes an effort to apply new ideas and change; he forces himself to do things that make him uncomfortable. It's unfortunate that he struggles so hard to get it right and that he alienates people even as he's trying to behave differently. Slowly, though, he's making progress. In the past, he would turn any confrontation into a verbal slugfest. Now, he's a little better at listening and responding without hostility.

It's a very difficult struggle for him to change and grow. But it's a healthy struggle. All of us have an innate drive toward growth despite the blockers that stand in our way. As long as you continue to respond to that drive and push yourself in the direction of growth, you'll eventually break through to greater levels of productivity and success.

As you begin to examine your past and search for your blockers, you'll find yourself entering the Internal

Frontier. As you do so, you'll discover that it's a bit scary to be in this unfamiliar territory. You're expected to take some risks, and this takes a certain amount of courage. Gaining clarity about who you are and where you're going can boost your confidence. That's why early in the process I've found it helpful to ask a series of nine questions. By providing your answers and comparing and contrasting them with the ones I've supplied, you should have a better sense of where you are in your own internal development.

CHAPTER 6

NINE QUESTIONS TO HELP YOU DRILL DOWN

As you've been reading, you naturally might have applied what you've read to your own life. It's likely that you've begun to consider what your *familiar* is. And if you've already started dealing with your contrast places and symbols in a growth relationship, you've brought some significant, yet scary, feelings to the surface.

To help you make some sense of these feelings and counter the misconceptions that might arise, I'd like you to answer the following nine questions. Write out your answers and refer to them, both when you've finished the book and later when you begin work on your own internal issues. They'll serve as a good baseline for your growth. Don't try to guess what the right answer is based on what you've read so far. Simply respond directly and honestly to the following:

1. **How do I help people in both their personal and professional lives deal with their problems, take on their challenges, and continue to grow and develop?**

   _____

   _____

   _____

2. What do I want out of the most important relationships in my life?

_____

_____

_____

_____

_____

3. Have some of my most important relation-ships gone sour? If so, why?

_____

_____

_____

_____

_____

4. How did I feel the last time I screwed up at work?

_____

_____

_____

_____

_____

5. Why haven't I achieved the goals I had when I was younger?

_____

_____

_____

_____

_____

6. How did I feel the last time I confronted someone about an important issue? How did I go about it?

_____

_____

_____

_____

_____

7. Do I ever feel really stuck in my job or in
   my personal life?

_____

_____

_____

_____

_____

8. What do I see in my job or my career that
   scares me to death?

_____

_____

_____

_____

_____

9. When I succeed at something and receive
   positive feedback, how do I respond?

_____

_____

_____

_____

_____

During the course of our work, we've asked a wide
variety of people these questions. Despite the range in
their personalities, ages, and levels of responsibility, they
have all responded with remarkably similar answers. You
probably did too. In the following pages, you'll find the
"conventional" response to each question and then the
unconventional "correct" response. The former comes
from people who reproduce the *familiar*, and the latter
from those who are aware of the *familiar* and are working
at creating a new, healthier one. As you read over these

questions and answers, think about why you responded as you did and the issues it raises in your life.

1. **How do I help people in both their personal and professional lives deal with their problems, take on their challenges, and continue to grow and develop?**

   CONVENTIONAL RESPONSE: *I help them by being highly supportive, particularly when they're having a difficult time. I usually back away from making them feel uncomfortable because it's not good for anyone. They get hurt and I feel guilty. Besides, by causing them discomfort I might ruin the relationship and lose any opportunity to help them change and grow.*

Most people choose to avoid causing discomfort, even though it's the single most powerful catalyst for people to take on new challenges with potentially higher payoffs. Discomfort triggers growth, forcing us to confront who we are and how who we are is keeping us stuck. Without discomfort, we invariably return to the *familiar*, which by definition is a more comfortable place to be. The problem is that when we return to the *familiar*, inertia sabotages our drive to develop and progress.

Growing and developing people is about learning. If we truly care about the people we work and live with, then we will feel committed to challenging them continually to learn more about themselves, others around them, and the world in which they live. What makes life exciting is learning, and learning—through relationships—provides the foundation for success. Only mediocre people have learned everything they need to know.

The mistake many people make is equating caring with comfort. We're taught to believe that if we really care about others, we'll go out of our way to keep them happy and satisfied, no matter what the price. And the price may well be the relationship itself, which is unlikely to endure a static, no-growth condition created by an obsessive clinging to the *familiar*.

Let's say you've just received your performance review. You're huddled in your supervisor's office, and things are going very well. "You're doing a great job," you're told. "We're really happy with you. Don't change anything. Just keep doing what you've been doing."

What's wrong with this picture? On the surface it's wonderful. But probe a little further, and it is not as positive as it seems. You're being told to stay the same, maintain the status quo, toe the line. That is unlikely to have a positive outcome for anyone. If you fail to change, you will not bring new ideas and fresh perspectives to your organization. Even worse, you won't augment your own resources and capabilities.

A generation or two ago, that might have been fine. In fact, until relatively recently people were more likely to build a career with a single employer. Companies were paternalistic and would teach employees a skill set that they could slowly develop to last throughout their career. Today this doesn't work. Chances are you'll have a number of jobs with a range of employers. Or you might change careers (and you might change them more than once). Or you might find yourself trying to cope with constantly changing policies, cultures, and opportunities. You can't meet any of these challenges if you're not continually growing and developing.

In other words, you can't afford to keep doing what you've been doing, and the supervisor who praises you for maintaining the status quo is damning you with faint praise indeed. What he's really doing is encouraging you to stay stuck in your *familiar*.

People don't grow and develop if no one challenges them about their negative behaviors and attitudes. It might be painful to confront someone (especially if that person is doing a good job in their area of technical training) whose constant office chatter is driving everyone crazy, or to point out that a subordinate's out-of-control personal life is causing her to be distracted and unproductive. But if we always tell people what they want to hear, we just perpetuate relationships that are comfortable but ultimately superficial and pointless. Telling people painful truths is the only way to build strong relationships that help others grow. If you question this, think about what would happen if the only goal of parenting were to make our children happy. If that's all parenting was about, our kids would never leave home, they would never learn how to develop relationships with different kinds of people, and they would be emotionally and professionally crippled.

The enormous popularity of consensus decision-making, mediation/negotiation, participatory management, and self-directed work teams is a sign of the times that is validating our unhealthy quest for comfort above all. The driving force behind all these concepts is the belief that unless everyone gets along and agrees about everything, we'll never be able to accomplish anything. According to this theory, confrontation and conflict are bad because they make people uncomfortable.

Our culture is obsessed with the notion that the point of life is to avoid its discomfort and to always be happy. The unhappy fact is that we've become a hedonistic society that stresses pleasure. We see the results every time we read about the latest celebrity who has fallen victim to alcoholism or drug addiction and is imprisoned, institutionalized, or dead in quest of the ultimate high. We've lost sight of the fact that we can't be happy all the time and that life includes unpleasant choices and other painful moments. The greatest sense of satisfaction we can achieve is fulfilling our potential by growing, developing, and facing painful issues that make us better and more fully realized people. If you only seek pleasure, you may be happy for a while. But you will soon tire of that short-term payoff and find yourself chronically unhappy, always having to up the ante to get that familiar feeling of comfort. The real opportunity lies in feeling a tremendous sense of accomplishment about getting to the next level of meaning and value in your life.

2. **What do I want out of the most important relationships in my life? What do I expect from my spouse, my family, my close friends, my work associates?**

CONVENTIONAL RESPONSE: *I want people who support me and what I want to do, who care about me and offer me positive reinforcement and validation at all times, who accept me for who I am no matter what I do. I want to fill my life with people who respect and love me unconditionally because of who I am, no matter what mistakes I make. I know I'll make mistakes, but my support network will always be there for me no matter what happens.*

One of the enduring themes in our culture is the transformational power of friendship and love. The novels we read and the movies we watch are replete with it.

In fact, one of the most popular movies ever made, *It's a Wonderful Life*, is about the head of a bankrupt small-town financial institution who is saved by the spiritual and economic support of his family and friends.

It's a great story and a very enjoyable film. But it's hogwash. If that situation were really to happen to you, your friends might be very sympathetic, but they probably are not going to be able to bail you out of a crisis that was created through your own irresponsibility, even if they were inclined to do so. All the friendship and love they can muster isn't likely to solve the problem for you. In the real world, they serve you much better if they help you avert the crisis in the first place. Real friends who care about you would observe your descent into self-pity and denial, and encourage you to solve the problems that were jeopardizing your business.

Of course, nobody takes the movies seriously. Everybody understands that this film and other popular entertainments are nothing more than sentimental fantasies. Or do they? We perceive intellectually that good fellowship, romance, and love are not likely to offer lasting solutions to our problems. But this concept is so pervasive, so thoroughly rooted in the public consciousness, that most of us do harbor an underlying belief in exactly that. A related illusion is that someone will recognize our talents and rescue our careers. We believe that parents, spouses, mentors, and other significant figures in our lives are capable of leading us out of the desert. It's very appealing and convenient to look for answers outside ourselves.

The thing we need to remember is that the only real source of achievement is inside every person. Our loved ones, friends, and associates—the people with whom we form growth relationships—can help us understand ourselves better and capitalize on the power we all have. But seeking unconditional support or salvation from a personal network—at the expense of developing and relying upon our own capacities as individuals—results in disappointment, failure, and dissatisfaction with ourselves.

3. Why have some of my most important relationships gone sour?

CONVENTIONAL RESPONSE: *When my relationships have turned bad, it was because the other person didn't come through for me. I expect people in my life to support me when things get tough. When I don't feel like I can depend on someone to back me one hundred percent, then the relationship is over. In many cases, I feel like I've worked overtime to support the other person and give them what they need, but they haven't responded in kind. To me, that's an unequal relationship.*

Relationships sour because of unequal rates of growth. When people get married, they often are at the same place in their lives, but after a period of years one person can easily outdistance the other. Mary and John, for instance, are a couple who divorced after twelve years of marriage. Mary is acutely aware of her internal issues and regularly takes internal risks in order to grow. John, on the other hand, has been stuck in the same place for years. Mary has progressed at her work as well, taking on a series of increasingly challenging positions. John is a high school teacher who has taught the same syllabus in the same way for more than a decade. It's not surprising that they got divorced; what's surprising is that they didn't do it sooner. Similarly, relationships end at work when two people follow different growth paths. When there's a falling out between coworkers, the underlying cause has nothing to do with "the failure to support" of the conventional response. Instead, it has everything to do with a failure on the part of one person to grow. While one person is expressing feelings and trying out new, risky behaviors, the other person is hiding feelings and repeating the same old behaviors. "You've changed," the no-growth person accuses. "You haven't," the high-growth person says, and that's the cause of the split.

In relationships, we get just what we bargained for. We choose spouses or find bosses or subordinates who reinforce our *familiar*. We mistake the comfortable feeling of the *familiar* for intimacy or a productive work relationship. It's only when one person begins to change and grow that the emptiness of the relationship is exposed.

Relationships also fall apart when you do a poor job of communicating what you need from a partner. An unhappy wife may say, "I want a divorce because you never meet my needs. I just want to know I'm cared about, to be shown some affection and concern. You never ask me questions about my day or my life. And when you do, they aren't the right questions."

Does she want a divorce because he never asks the right questions? Or is it really that he failed to give her life the meaning she had sought from the relationship? If there is something missing from her life and she feels she contributes little to anyone or anything, no individual other than her has the power to change that. Instead of looking to her husband for answers, she needs to be looking to him for feedback, and both need to be looking to each other for some challenge and accountability in order to break through their inertia.

Indifference, rather than hate, is the cause of relationships falling apart. When we love or hate, we are emotionally engaged and passionate. Indifference is destructive because it returns us to our *familiars*. Being alone is part of the human condition. Our fear of being isolated, on the other hand, comes from having no one to share our feelings with, and no one who genuinely listens to us. This fear drives us to frenetic activity in a desperate attempt to connect emotionally. Spouses become overly demonstrative and clingy to breathe life back into a marriage, and subordinates annoy their bosses with bizarre antics designed to capture their attention. These feelings and tactics are familiar and eventually backfire, and end the relationship sooner rather than later. The only way to save these relationships is for both people to be open and vulnerable and deal with their internal issues first.

4. How did I feel the last time I screwed up at work?

CONVENTIONAL RESPONSE: *When my work has been criticized, it's usually because I was not adequately informed about what was expected of me or because the assignment changed in midstream. I'm not a mind reader, so if someone doesn't tell me exactly what's needed or if circumstances alter the need and I'm not informed, then I won't satisfy the goals of the assignment. Though the person who gave me the assignment is clearly at fault, I still get frustrated and feel like I've failed. Sometimes I avoid the person I've disappointed, and I even question my role and my future at the company.*

People who have not done their Internal Frontier work and are reproducing the *familiar* either blame others for their mistake or feel like their screwup is the end of the world. If you can accept responsibility for your error or not let the behavior of others distract you from your goals, then you've done a good job of diluting the power of your *familiar*.

You know that you've fallen into your *familiar* when you become fearful that the botched assignment or missed deadline is an irrevocable error. You feel that you'll never recover from it. If you're frightened enough, the only way you can handle the fear is by absolving yourself and blaming someone else. Stuck in your *familiar*, you might even deepen the crisis by avoiding the person you disappointed, who then may become even more upset with you because you never seem to be around. Massive overreaction comes with this territory. Managers become more and more angry with subordinates for messing up, and subordinates become more and more angry with managers for not being clear about what they expect. Because neither party expresses their feelings to the other, the anger builds.

The current business environment fosters unproductive responses to failures. In the past, there were more people and more time to throw at tasks. There was more room for error, and it was easier to forgive one. Today, the competitive pressures are so intense that bosses are far less tolerant of screwups. These pressures not only make mistakes more visible, but they increase the odds that you'll react in a familiar way. Let's say your employer is considering an acquisition of another company, and your boss says: "I need you to develop a report on the Wonderful Widgets Corporation. Include the location of all the operations, annual revenues, all the products it manufactures, and other important facts about the company."

After reading your report, your boss hands it back and tells you, "That's not what I need! You left out the most important piece of information: the compensation and benefit packages of the top management group. How are we going to get a handle on the company if we don't know the financial drivers of the key officers of the company?"

This response flings you back to your *familiar:* "I always felt like I let people down when I was a kid, and now I'm letting my boss down. What I felt then was anger and frustration, and I stewed about my mistakes, and that's exactly how I feel now." Instead of simply acknowledging the omission and obtaining the requested information, you get sidetracked in resentment, blaming, or feeling incompetent. You overreact, waste time fretting, and cause your boss to be even more disappointed with you than he was before. You begin to hate him and hate your job and think, "I don't need this."

To respond effectively when you fall short of someone else's expectations, you need to focus on keeping the present reality separate and distinct from the past *familiar.* In the present, you probably fell short for a combination of reasons: You should have realized that executive compensation and benefits are critical factors in an acquisition, and you should have had a very specific pro forma for doing the report. In terms of "fault," both you and your boss are culpable. But fault is not the issue here. In the present, you—and hopefully your boss—learned something. It's only your *familiar* that makes it seem like a major catastrophe.

5. Why haven't I achieved the goals I had when I was younger?

CONVENTIONAL RESPONSE: *I never really seemed to get the right opportunity. If I had an advanced degree from the right school, I'd be further along in my career by now. I also think that if I came from a family with the right connections, I would have had more opportunities to advance faster. Or maybe I just wasn't in the right place at the right time. Sometimes I feel that my best efforts are doomed to failure, that I have some fatal flaw that always makes me fall short no matter how hard I try. But I think I've done what I could, given the obstacles I've faced.*

Most people who have fallen substantially short of their goals look outside themselves for answers. They believe they never got a break or they have some mysterious Achilles' heel—"There's something about me that is hindering me, and I can't get past it." In most cases, the only real obstacle lies within. Just as we establish goals on our own—often at a very tender age—we fail to reach them on our own because we didn't do the things they required. If you want to be a doctor but don't get into your first choice of medical school, why don't you apply to some others? There are lots of medical schools. And if every single one has rejected you, why don't you enhance your credentials and reapply? *You* determine whether you meet your goals. Have you been in important jobs that hold you to a high standard of performance, or have you sought jobs that are undemanding? Have you searched for relationships in which you were held accountable, or have you gone after relationships where everything you did was acceptable?

Non-goal achievers do achieve one thing: a comfortable feeling of mediocrity. Mired in that mediocrity, they look for external scapegoats for their lack of achievement.

Some women and members of ethnic minorities complain that discrimination is standing in the way of their goals. But if that's true, why are so many women and minorities advancing to unprecedented levels of responsibility and income? If you want to achieve what they have, ask yourself, "What are they doing that I'm not?" The answer usually is that they broke free from that comfortable feeling of mediocrity and found jobs and relationships that challenged them and that catalyzed their growth.

This is not to say that discrimination is a thing of the past; clearly it still exists and hurts people. But if your firm is one that makes it impossible to advance because of your color, your ethnicity, or for any other reason, why are you still there? It's difficult for any of us to convince ourselves that there is one and only one company who will employ us. It's easy to believe, however, that your *familiar* is being in a situation where people don't accept you for who you are and you're going to get them to like you if it kills both of you. You know how to deal with being rejected. What's scary is feeling uncomfortable in a new environment where you are accepted, but more is demanded of you (and where the rewards are greater).

Many myths around goals have arisen in our culture, and one of the most powerful among them is that people who achieve great goals have powers beyond the reach of mortal men and women. They have the "right stuff," and the rest of us don't. This is absurd. People aren't genetically programmed to succeed. Most individuals who succeed and achieve ambitious goals do so because they've taken the risk of experiencing unfamiliar things. Think about how many times in your life you've backed away from a major opportunity because of your fear of the unfamiliar. Most of us have done it. Perhaps you didn't want to go to the prestigious school that accepted you because it seemed far more challenging than your small-town high school. Or maybe you turned down a great job because it seemed like it would be too much work and there would be too much pressure put on you.

It's much easier to blame a lack of connections, bad timing, or our own inherent "failure gene" than it is to get in touch with our internal issues and break with the *familiar*.

6. How did I feel the last time I confronted someone about an important issue? How did I go about it?

CONVENTIONAL RESPONSE: *It was very unpleasant, and I still feel terrible about what happened. A junior person had missed two deadlines on a very important project, and the client became upset with me, so I took it out on my subordinate. I was frustrated, and I really tore into him. He was very hurt and resentful, and the guy hasn't been the same since. I think I shook his confidence and may have cost the company a good employee. I wish I could control my temper in these situations, but the guy really let me down.*

Most people hate confrontation or handle it poorly if they haven't dealt with their *familiar*. As a child, you may have been a figurative punching bag for a parent's frustration with his lack of success; Dad yelled at you all the time. Or you may have learned that the only way to survive was to give as good as you got. Whatever your past might have been, confrontation often triggers overreactions or underreactions. You're no longer dealing with an issue in the present, but an unresolved one from your past.

One of the biggest problems people have with confrontation is an inability to differentiate anger from hostility. Hostility often manifests itself in a personal attack that expands from a specific incident to an indictment of the target's entire character. "You idiot!" the boss shouts. "How could you have been so stupid as to forget to include the CEO in the memo?" Such a hostile overreaction has more to do with the past than the present. This is as opposed to exhibiting healthy anger at someone for making a mistake and confronting him by saying, "I'm disappointed that you didn't realize we need to include the CEO in our meetings, and I hope you won't make the same mistake again."

Undealt-with issues can also cause you to confront others halfheartedly and soften the impact. You might be scared to death of expressing your disappointment, so you drop vague hints: "I had a discussion with Susan, and I subtly suggested that she do things a little differently next time. I didn't really criticize her directly, but I'm sure she put two and two together and got the message." Probably not. Because you haven't expressed your disappointment clearly, Susan doesn't have any idea that she should do things differently and will continue to work ineffectively.

7. Do I ever feel really stuck in my job or in my personal life?

CONVENTIONAL RESPONSE: *I do feel stuck, and it seems that I can't get out of my rut. I've tried a lot of things—different jobs, different relationships—but it seems that I always end up with jobs and relationships that ultimately are unsatisfying. I'd like to change things, but it seems that this is the best I can expect. I just don't know how to do things differently.*

A seductive aspect of the *familiar* is that it encourages you to remain stuck. By definition, the *familiar* is anti-change. It causes you to act in ways that make you feel the same way you always have. If you take a risk and try something new that results in personal growth, the feeling is scary and strange. Thus, you avoid it and remain as mediocre as ever, waiting for the world to act upon you. Perhaps as a child you waited for someone to show interest in you and no one did. So you've been waiting ever since for something to happen that never will.

Childhood and adolescence are natural waiting periods, when we begin to learn how to fend for ourselves before we're ready to leave the nest. But when we reach adulthood, we lose the right to keep waiting. To be effective adults, we need to chart a course that takes us away from our *familiars* into new, stimulating, and productive directions. It's about assuming risk, and the greatest risk is asking someone to participate in a relationship that demands that you grow and develop in new directions. You could fail or be rejected, and in the back of your mind an insistent voice is saying, "I told you so; stick with what you know."

We've worked with successful executives who struggle with something as elementary as calling a store to complain that the new computer they just bought doesn't work. They say to themselves: "I'm stuck with the damn thing." Some people react the same way to the Fifth Wave world. It overwhelms people and makes them feel like anachronisms. They think the world has changed much too quickly and that they're hopelessly out of touch; it's too late to do anything to give their lives value.

You probably know people who are overwhelmed by the Information Age, who think that it is fine for young kids who grew up with computers but that they're too far behind to catch up.

The *familiar* also causes people to feel a profound sense of shame about their needs. If you grew up in an environment where the message your family sent was that you shouldn't expect too much, then as an adult it somehow feels wrong to want too much (in other words, to want much of anything). You think you should have modest needs, and that if you want more you should feel guilty. That's what makes it easy to accept what you have and become stuck. At many organizations, you find at least one person on the management team who is highly talented and makes great contributions to the company but is relatively low-paid. He's angry at those who make much more money and a far smaller contribution. But rather than demanding more money, he complains about the people who are overpaid, an issue that is beyond his control. He can advocate for issues and causes. He can even champion other people's interests and needs. What he finds almost impossible to do is to demand (or even request) that *his* needs be met. The message he got growing up was: "Be grateful for what you have because other people have nothing. Don't be selfish."

If you don't address issues such as this one—if you don't identify the *familiar* in your life—you'll be stuck in a job or career that ensures mediocrity and dissatisfaction.

8. What do I see in my job or my career that scares me to death?

CONVENTIONAL RESPONSE: *The thing that scares me the most is that I've learned everything I can from this job and that the boredom I feel now will last the rest of my career. But if I tell my superiors, they might tell me that it's time for me to leave. My greatest fear is that I'm finished with my current employer, but I don't know what to do next.*

For most people, the real fear is confronting someone about their situation. If you admit you're bored and say you need a change, your boss might say, "You've got a great deal. I'm paying you a lot, you're doing a good job, and I need you to keep doing it."

If you grew up in a home where your parents had achieved as much as they thought they could, your boss's familiar response would feel familiar. Your family shut you down when you demanded something from them; such a demand would have forced them to grow. The words "that's your problem, not mine" signal their refusal to listen to that demand. What's familiar to you is feeling like you were shut down then and you'll be shut down now.

Demands are scary for many adults. I have a fifteen-year-old son who was caught smoking at school. When Arleah and I were informed by the school of his infraction, we blew up at him. He told us, "I know what I did was stupid. I don't know why I do things like that and I'll take responsibility for them. But both of you are overreacting, it's way out of proportion to what happened, and I think you should look at that." Spoken like the son of two therapists. But he had a point. After I got past my initial anger—"What right does this snot-nosed kid have telling me about what I should look at?"—I realized he was right and admitted he was. This was very difficult to do; he was putting the demand on me to look at why I was so triggered by this behavior. It would have been much easier to be angry at him and not examine my own issues.

When you have a healthy, growing work relationship, each person should place demands on the other, and these demands facilitate growth and change. But if it's a relationship where people don't express their feelings (and aren't in touch with them), demands are frightening both to hear and to make.

It's interesting to note that organizations are just as scared of demanding things from their people as individuals are. One organization we work with has gone through some tough times recently. Their response to falling revenues has been to look at various acquisitions. A more effective response would be to confront their internal processes and their people and to demand more from both. It's difficult to confront poor performers and a flawed organization and ask more of them for many reasons, not the least of which is management's fear that employees will make a reciprocal demand for better processes and clearer relationships from the organization. Acquiring is a convenient way to avoid facing this scary prospect.

9. When I succeed at something and receive positive feedback, how do I respond?

CONVENTIONAL RESPONSE: *I celebrate my success. It's the greatest feeling in the world. It's highly motivating, and I can't wait to jump into the next project with even more responsibility and a potentially greater payoff.*

I wish it were that simple. Our experience is that goal achievement and success create an initial high, followed by a difficulty in refocusing and a period of plateauing and inactivity. The feelings that accompany this place are often ones of boredom, disappointment, and sadness—a sense of generalized letdown and lack of fulfillment.

Our society embraces the notion of success as a panacea. If you have success, you have it all. In fact, when you succeed, you break away from the *familiar*. Every bit of success breaks old patterns. Let's say your *familiar* is feeling like everything good in life comes only after tremendous struggle. Suddenly, you're finding that it's getting easier and easier to succeed. When you land a big account or swing a major deal with relatively little effort, that's an uncomfortable, unfamiliar feeling. It's a feeling you may try to avoid, at least in the near future. Mediocrity and slow, incremental advancement are much more comfortable for you.

What stops people in their careers is not that they've gone as far as they can go, but that they've gone as far as their *familiar* will allow. They're scared of another big success because when they achieve it, they won't know who they are anymore.

If you'll recall, I described the dark and empty feeling that follows success as a contrast place, which can block us from further growth. When each of us achieves a significant goal and people praise us for it, we're thrown back to a time when we did something well and our accomplishments weren't appreciated or even acknowledged. Subconsciously, we're asking ourselves: Why couldn't the people back then appreciate me the way people do now? The contrast between present reality and past feelings is terribly sad. Intellectually, we understand we should celebrate success. Emotionally, however, success engenders a mixed bag of feelings. Some of these feelings are connected to our familiar places, and identifying these past *familiars* is a prerequisite to fully enjoying our present success.

THERE ARE NO RIGHT ANSWERS

The point of this chapter is not to make you feel inadequate or to demonstrate what an awful past you had. As we've emphasized before, all of us who grow up in even the most "normal" of families are given issues to deal with. If we ignore them, we reproduce the *familiar* and are likely to provide the conventional responses discussed in this chapter.

The goal here is to help you to begin personalizing the themes of this book. When you think about how you answered the questions, you can begin to address larger questions of growth and change in your own life. You can identify the underlying problems that are limiting your effectiveness and success. You can think about your relationships and determine if they're growth-oriented.

If you found yourself providing the conventional response to each question, you now have a path to learning about your *familiar*. If you agonize and beat yourself up, that may tell you a lot about what you've carried forward from your past. It means that you haven't yet made all the connections between personal transformation and professional success. The following chapters will provide you with process tools and techniques for making these connections.

CHAPTER 7

DIMINISHING THE POWER OF THE OLD *FAMILIARS*

Finding the *familiar* and then creating a new one isn't a haphazard process. It doesn't happen overnight, nor does it happen without continuous work. As the previous chapters suggest, powerful obstacles prevent us from recognizing our *familiar* and doing something about its impact on our lives.

This chapter and the following three will help you explore your Internal Frontier by providing you with a better sense of what is involved, as well as how to use the process effectively. It's one thing to ask you to identify your *familiar;* it's something else to give you a systematic way of doing so.

The following is a six-step system or process that will help you move from your old *familiar* to a healthier new *familiar:*

- Identifying repetitive feelings.
- Tracing the feelings backward in time.
- Expressing your feelings without blame or forgiveness.
- Allowing yourself to experience the sadness and anger that expressing your feelings engenders.

- Taking increasing risks to break the hold of the *familiar*.
- Creating a new *familiar* that redirects your energy.

REPETITIVE FEELINGS

In the first chapter, you'll recall the "find the *familiar*" exercise that asked you to choose the correct *familiar* from four alternatives. If you're like most people, you probably made an incorrect choice. It's very easy to misperceive the *familiar* as a behavior rather than a feeling, or fail to drill down deep enough in order to discover the primary emotion. You might want to review that earlier exercise before going forward.

To search for your *familiar*, start with a simple question:

> *What feelings are repetitive in my life, especially those attached to not succeeding, being disappointed, or not getting what I want?*

Then follow it up with questions such as:

- *What was my reaction to not getting into my first choice of colleges?*
- *How did I feel when I discovered that my current job wasn't exactly how I thought it would be?*
- *What were my feelings about getting dumped in a relationship that I was sure had a tremendous future?*

In answering these questions, it's very easy to mistake a secondary or tertiary response for a primary feeling. For instance, if I ask you how it makes you feel when your boss nitpicks your work and constantly criticizes your performance, you respond, "I feel angry."

Anger is a secondary emotion. To get at the primary feeling, we need to ask: Why were you angry? You might respond: "I was mad because when he hired me he promised I'd be judged on how well I met my major objectives and not if there were typos in my reports. I'm really disappointed that he broke his promise." Why were you disappointed? Because you *feel* hurt.

Hurt or pain is one of five primary feelings. The other four are *joy, fear, sadness,* and *grief/loss.* Whenever you can ask another "why" question about a response, then you're not yet at the primary feeling. If you respond, "I feel frustrated about the situation," you're merely describing an intellectual concept. Why did you feel frustrated? Because you were hurt.

When people attempt to identify the repetitive feelings in their lives, they gravitate toward "safer" intellectual responses. Our parents may have discouraged us from expressing some or all of the five primary feelings. It's also hard for businesspeople—especially men—to say they're hurt or in emotional pain. They are much more likely to tell people they're furious, they don't understand, they don't care, or they're confused. Hurt, however, is a feeling you don't hear people express very often.

TRACKING BACKWARD

Tracing a repetitive feeling back to its source usually can't be done instantly. At first, you might find it difficult to remember the childhood experiences that gave rise to your *familiars.* It often helps to create a "reverse time line" of the instances when you experienced your familiar feeling, starting with the most recent situation and working backward in time. Most people can remember back to young adulthood or adolescence. When we ask our clients to push back further, they tend to search for a cataclysmic event that will "explain everything." They seize on their parents' divorce, an instance of childhood abuse, or a death in the family. In most cases, these singular events aren't what people should be looking for. Don't focus on something that happened when you were an adolescent. The *familiar* is rooted in pedestrian, repetitive experiences that occur earlier, when children are malleable and impressionable.

For instance, a child may have proudly shown his father something he drew or made, and his father usually responded with "That's fine, but I'm kind of busy right now. Run along and play," or words and behaviors to that effect. If this only happens once or twice, it won't have much of an impact. But if it happens most of the time, it's highly impactful.

Another common example of these repetitive pedestrian experiences involves kids who never felt that people, usually their parents, were comfortable holding them. They can recall a number of times when Mom or Dad held them as kids and they sensed their parents were awkward and uncomfortable. As adults, these people are often involved in relationships where they'll make any compromise in order to have someone hold them in a loving way. At its worst, this *familiar* translates into people becoming involved with inappropriate lovers (the successful female executive who has an affair with the dull-as-a-doorknob mailroom clerk or the successful male executive who dates the empty-headed high school dropout).

While people are often able to remember repetitive childhood experiences by working backward on a time line, you may also want to consult siblings, relatives, or friends who can remind you of what happened. Be aware, however, that some of these people will be threatened by your questions and resist this exercise, saying something like, "You're nuts; you had a great childhood; I don't know what you're talking about."

As you look backward, focus on a common feeling rather than a common set of experiences. While it's possible that the same experience happened time after time, it's more likely that there were a variety of experiences that all produced the same feeling. You may also find that you recall more than one feeling; one series of experiences made you feel sadly alone and abandoned, another set created a deep sense of hurt, while a third set left you with a tremendous sense of loss. To locate your *familiar*, it helps to keep two things in mind:

1. Sadness is a primary emotion, and feeling as if your needs weren't met and you were abandoned is often a telltale sign of the *familiar*. Anger and frustration are secondary emotions and mask primary ones.
2. It's important to emphasize that the goal of this process of pushing backward is to identify the feelings from your *past* that are familiar and are identical to what you often feel in the present. The feelings, in both the past and the present, are the same. The hurt you feel from a zinger in a business meeting is experienced no differently from having your attempts to contribute to a family discussion rebuffed. What *is* different

are the choices you have about responding to that feeling and the impact the feeling has on the rest of your life. In the past, there was no one around to share your hurt with (and no other options to pursue). This had a profound and widespread impact on the direction of your life. In the present, a hostile rebuff is a transitory hurt and leaves you with a multiplicity of choices, ranging from expressing your feelings to confronting the other person to working to change your environment. Your feelings don't change. But your responses to them can be dramatically altered.

EXPRESSING YOUR FEELINGS WITHOUT BLAMING OR FORGIVENESS

Sometimes people go about this search for the *familiar* as if they were detectives, and when they find the "culprit," they start blaming. "I would be a lot further along in my career if it weren't for all the baggage my parents saddled me with" or "I can't assert myself because my family never was successful at anything, and that's the *familiar* for me so I can't go any further than that."

Acknowledgment and acceptance of your feelings are what's important; blaming will only get you stuck in the past. Some people take the opposite approach and magnanimously forgive everyone for everything. This forgiveness is just another way of not dealing with these issues. Rather than feel the sadness and disappointment they experienced, these forgivers engage in an elaborate form of denial—forgiveness allows them to pretend that what they experienced as children had no real impact on their lives.

Rather than blame or forgive, the next step in the process is to express our feelings. Only when we express how we feel are we able to leave the feeling behind. This doesn't mean that you have to get on a plane, fly home to Mom, and tell her how sad you feel because she ignored you as a child. This has nothing do with the other person (or persons) and everything to do with you. Articulating a feeling that has lain dormant for years is the key.

There are all sorts of ways to do this, including:

- *Writing a letter.* Express your feelings in writing to a parent, grandparent, or some other meaning-ful person in your early life about how disap-pointed you were with them. There's no need to send the letter; you just have to write it.
- *Visiting the cemetery.* If the person who served as a symbol in your life has died, one effective way of expressing your feelings is to visit the gravesite and say what you have to say in that environment.
- *Talking to a spouse or other significant person in your life.* It doesn't matter if your wife, best friend, or work colleague never met the person from your past. As long as you've established a trusting, open relationship with this person in your present, you can express how you felt to him or her.

Other ways to articulate feelings include journal-ing, crying, and carving out private time for yourself to reflect and "be" with your feelings.

PREPARE YOURSELF TO CYCLE THROUGH THE GRIEVING PROCESS

Once you surface your feelings, you'll be able to grieve them and what you've lost. This is emotionally healthy, but it also produces a variety of disturbing feelings. One day you'll wake up feeling miserable for no particular reason. Another day you might feel inexplicably sad. It's important to accept that you can't control all these feelings, turning them on and off when it's convenient. They just arrive, and you need to give yourself permission to experience them. Most people don't give themselves that permission, especially busy, high-achieving professionals. Instead, they try to "fix" this response, not only in themselves but in others. They say or think: "Snap out of it, you were just promoted, there's no reason on earth you should feel sad." It's the same thing parents do when their children are sad and disappointed. Instead of accepting a child's right to feel bad about something that's happened, they try to distract the child, shifting the focus away from these feelings. They give kids suggestions about how they might feel better; they say that even though their best friend was mean to them, they'll all go out for ice cream and that will make them happy.

It's important for you to understand that you need to deal with your feelings in two ways. Expressing the feeling is one way, and experiencing the feeling is the second. Perhaps this seems like a fine distinction, but it is a significant distinction nonetheless. Expressing means bringing the feeling to the surface in some way—writing a letter, talking about it, and so on. Experiencing it means bringing the feeling back inside yourself and letting it wash over you without putting up any resistance or defenses. You're experiencing it in the purest sense, and that helps dilute the power of the *familiar*. Together, the expression and the experience of feelings help you move through the stages of grief.

It's not only sadness that you feel after expressing your feelings, but anger or even rage. This is the second stage of grief, and one day you'll wake up feeling angry at the world for no apparent reason. When this happens, ask yourself if there's anything in the present that's causing this reaction. If you had a pretty good week, then you can assume the catalyst for your rotten mood is in the distant past. It's a waste of energy to try to figure out what made you so angry on this particular day. If necessary, tell the people you work with that you happen to be in a lousy mood and that it doesn't have anything to do with them. Just allow yourself to be angry and accept it. The next time this feeling comes, it won't be quite as intense.

In your work environment, you need to prepare yourself for your overreaction, caused by the familiar feeling you've identified and expressed. Just being aware of a tendency to overreact when a situation throws you back to your *familiar* is crucial. For instance, when people disappoint the CEO we've discussed in previous chapters, he immediately returns to how he felt when he was with his alcoholic father. Now he knows that his first reaction to disappointment is a temper tantrum: A voice in his head screams, "Why did you do that to me?" and he wants to strike back. With his awareness of how he overreacts, however, this CEO often is able to control this response, back off, and deal with his disappointment in a more productive manner.

Like this CEO, we need to expand our repertoire of responses. Most of us become stuck in responding only one way to situations. It's not that we want to eliminate this response completely from our repertoire—sometimes it's appropriate to respond angrily, for instance—but to add other options. Self-awareness helps us expand our options.

The best way of preparing yourself for this overreaction is to make yourself acutely aware of the patterns and repetitive behaviors you fall into at work. What is your common response to situations in which you frequently find yourself? Let's say you're in sales. When you make a presentation, prospects frequently compliment you on your great ideas, but say that they can't afford to do what you've proposed. Your typical follow-up is to offer a weak argument for your concept, and when that doesn't work, you tell them you'll contact them later. You leave the presentation defeated, believing that no matter what you do, it's an exercise in futility.

How does it feel to get turned down by someone who says, "You're asking for too much and I can't give it to you"? It feels disappointing, of course. It's quite possible you react with shame: "I shouldn't have asked them to buy this in the first place." Or you may feel that you were too demanding and should have made the price more affordable from the start.

All this is tremendously familiar to you: feeling disappointed because you were asking for too much. It's the pattern in your work life, and it's the pattern in your home life. Identifying this pattern of repetitive behaviors is an important step in the process. Now that you're aware of the pattern, you can attempt to break it.

Let's say that instead of putting up a feeble argument in response to the prospect saying he can't afford it, you respond as follows: "I'm really disappointed. I really felt you were with me on this until we started talking about money. You know, I've found that money is hardly ever an obstacle to closing a deal. Usually, there's something that's missing from the relationship. What's missing for you that would allow us to move forward with this proposal?"

What you're doing is upping the ante. You're challenging the prospect to provide feedback about how the deal might turn out differently. This is a tremendously unfamiliar feeling for you: You're demanding more. You're taking a risk by communicating to the prospect that his uninformative rejection is unacceptable.

One of two things will happen. The prospect might say, "Didn't you hear me? I said it was too much, now get out of here!" The prospect is clearly communicating that he doesn't want to have a relationship with you, and that he views your interaction purely as a transaction. That's good to know. It tells you that you were dealing with the wrong person, and it's time to move on and identify prospects who want something more sustainable than a hit-and-run encounter. We've worked with thousands of sales professionals, and we've found that they often deal with prospects who fit right into their *familiar*—they will provide that familiar feeling of being shot down when they ask for something. Salespeople drain the same well and cultivate non-clients, not simply because prospecting is hard, but primarily because leaving behind the *familiar* of rejection and disappointment is scary and disorienting. We teach them to qualify prospects in a new way: Are they the sort of people who are closed, transaction artists, or are they open people looking to form relationships?

The second way a prospect might respond is by sharing information about what's important to his company and what he expects from suppliers; he might start asking you questions about your approach to customers.

This doesn't mean that you'll necessarily make this sale. What it can mean, however, is that you'll develop a relationship that could pay off down the road.

In one sense, however, it doesn't matter how the prospect reacts. The point is for you to take the risk of asking for more. Asking for more is at the heart of personal transformation and professional breakthroughs. This is how you start to create a new *familiar*. The real risk is asking for more than you asked for in the past, recognizing that it's only "more" to some people and not others. It might have been too much for someone from your past. It might be too much for someone who only cares about transactions. But it's not too much for someone who values relationships.

STARTING SMALL AND ESCALATING THE RISK

Just because you're aware of the destructive patterns you've fallen into at work, and the familiar feeling you reproduce, doesn't mean you can instantly break its hold. Creating a new *familiar* is a gradual, incremental process, as the following two stories demonstrate.

Harriet was an administrative assistant who was scared to give her boss feedback, especially when he made mistakes. Harriet had been covering up these mistakes for years, and she'd never tell him that he sent a letter to the wrong person or copied someone on a memo who no longer worked for the company. Harriet was a fixer; she would take care of things. Her *familiar* was about feeling small and powerless; it was how her dad made her feel when she dared to correct him for something he did wrong.

Harriet went through the process described in this chapter and began taking small risks. At first, she simply told her boss about grammatical mistakes he made in his letters, and she lived to tell the tale. Then she escalated the risk, explaining to him that he was directing his correspondence to the wrong people and that this could make him look bad in the eyes of company leaders. Over time, Harriet was able to confront him about major errors he was making that could jeopardize both of their positions.

Jack's boss treats him rudely, frequently making denigrating remarks, throwing pieces of paper at him, and generally acting as if Jack is worthless. When we began working with Jack, we asked him if he ever confronted his boss about these behaviors, and Jack was horrified at even the suggestion that he confront him; he was sure that if he ever brought up these issues, his volatile boss would explode.

As we worked with Jack and he began to see that his terror had more to do with his past than his present, he was willing to confront his boss about a relatively minor issue: He told him that he thought it was unprofessional to throw pieces of paper at him and that it made it difficult for him to work effectively. Jack was amazed when his boss took this comment pretty well and said he'd try to stop throwing anything at him.

Jack escalated his risk a notch a few weeks later when he asked his boss to slow down and explain assignments in more detail rather than tossing them on his desk and saying that they were "self-explanatory." Jack explained that he could do a better job if his boss took a little more time to review what he wanted. Again, his boss didn't explode; he agreed to do what Jack requested.

Jack kept escalating his risk, telling his boss that the way he snapped at him and cut him to ribbons with cruel criticisms was undermining their relationship. His boss apologized. Of course, his boss still lost his temper on occasion, but not as often or with the same invective. It's important to point out that Jack's boss didn't react to these confrontations with joy and appreciation. He was most often sullen and only begrudgingly responsive. What is critical is that the boss's reaction was not as devastating as Jack's *familiar* had led him to predict, and that Jack's reaction was not what he expected from himself.

In essence, Jack created a different response to an old stimulus. This is a good definition of a new *familiar*. Instead of sulking for an hour when his boss snaps at him, because that was how Jack dealt with getting yelled at when he was a kid, Jack is able to wait ten minutes, knock on his boss's door, and discuss his feelings about how his boss treated him. Instead of sulking and becoming stuck in his old feelings, he moves on and goes back to work.

Creating a new *familiar* doesn't banish the old one. Certain things will still trigger these old feelings. They won't, however, be of the same doomsday intensity. People won't feel like their life is over, that they can't do anything right, or that they're worthless. Instead, they merely become uncomfortable and recognize the need to do something about it immediately.

This new *familiar* isn't a panacea. If Jack's boss was a nutcase, he might have responded to Jack by screaming bloody murder when Jack confronted him. But even if Jack's boss never yells at him again, his old *familiar* will be triggered by someone else in different and unpredictable ways.

You can significantly impact other people, but you can't change them. As you yourself change, however, you interact differently and don't set up the old responses as often. You can do this by taking on your own *familiar*. Your goal, therefore, is to react to people differently and in ways that make you more productive and successful.

BREAKTHROUGH ENERGY

The Internal Frontier is a place where your energy is redirected. This process results in tremendous gains in productivity and effectiveness because it frees your energy to work toward important goals. Typically, people waste most of their energy protecting themselves from old *familiars*. It's squandered on worrying about "How am I going to tell my boss the bad news?" or agonizing over a range of relatively easy decisions. It requires a great deal of energy to keep up these emotional fences and prevent new, uncomfortable feelings from entering. When you ask someone a question and he says, "It's none of your business," you become stuck for hours, even days, fretting and fuming about how no one respects you and everyone treats you like dirt. When you go through the process of exploring your Internal Frontier, however, you're able to move past the feelings the "none of your business" remark triggers and get on with what your business really is. Your energy is focused on building relationships and achieving goals rather than holding on to your familiar need to know everything.

If you examine any work environment, you'll find many people who are wasting their energy on unproductive behaviors and feelings. Ironically, they're often the busiest people in their organizations. They move around in an unfocused frenzy, working hard only to protect themselves from feelings they don't want to have. There's a senior manager I've worked with who has superior analytical abilities, but when he sits down with his people, he never asks them how they feel about the feedback he gives them. Instead, he's flying from one crisis to the next and never has enough time for anyone or anything. This senior manager wouldn't be in this constant state of hyperactivity if he simply took a few minutes and talked to his people about how they feel about the demands placed upon them. By allowing them to express how they feel, he'd free up some of their energy and help them accomplish tasks that he's running around like a madman trying to accomplish on his own. Unfortunately, he grew up in a home where people never talked about how they felt, and the last thing he wants to do now is hear all that nasty, messy stuff.

Enormous amounts of energy are wasted in meetings that all organizations routinely have. They're often an elaborate ballet of people reproducing their *familiars*, one after the other. Many meetings are nothing more than endless chatter about trivial subjects, vituperative exchanges, defensive soliloquies, and overlong apologies ("I hope what I'm about to say doesn't offend you, so I'd like to start out by giving you a sense of why I'm going to say what I'm about to say . . ."). All this unfocused activity results in very little progress toward meaningful goals.

When we avoid confronting core issues and expressing our feelings directly and honestly, we waste energy in all sorts of ways. When I recently recommended not promoting a senior executive who worked for a company I've consulted with, the executive was furious with me. Rather than tell me how he felt, however, he worked hard to avoid me. It was virtually impossible for me to track him down and get him to respond to important questions or make key decisions. When we were thrown together in a meeting, he was painfully polite. When we talked, we ended up talking around issues because he was terrified of opening up the real issue and allowing all his stored venom to come pouring out. I heard from others that he was blaming me for problems in areas of the company that I had no contact with or responsibility for. It was draining for both of us, and I finally took him aside and talked to him about this painful issue. I explained that I respected and liked him but simply didn't feel he was ready for the higher-level position. I said I was uncomfortable with his hostility, and that we needed to move beyond that because it made it difficult for us to work together productively. I made a point of telling him that it was perfectly appropriate for him to be angry with me and disappointed with my recommendation. Further, expressing his anger toward me directly was a lot more productive and a whole lot better for our relationship than carrying an unspoken grudge. After talking about it, the relationship improved considerably and we weren't wasting so much time dancing around each other.

DIFFERENT RESPONSES TO THE PROCESS

People transition from old to new *familiars* with varying degrees of speed and difficulty. Some people are very open and willing to examine and express their feelings. Others are terrified of doing so and put up great resistance to the process. The response often has to do with how much their *familiar* relates to being perfect. When I give feedback to these individuals, I can see them become tense and begin to close up. It's as if they believe I've discovered something terribly wrong with them and they'll never be able to recover from my discovery. They resist like crazy when anyone points out any area they need to work on; they feel like any criticism shows them up as frauds and failures.

Recently I was working with three young managers, all of whom had difficulty confronting their people. When I discussed the problem with them, two of the managers reacted defensively and resisted what I was saying. The third manager, however, absorbed the input eagerly. He relished talking about how he felt and hearing feedback about how others felt about him. Because his issues didn't revolve around being perfect—as a child, his parents rarely made him feel like he had to be perfect—he took to the process much more readily than the other managers.

Whether you find this process easy or difficult, it's important to work through the process in a relationship. Reading this book and thinking about the issues it raises is great, but you need to involve someone else or you'll lose perspective and become frustrated and stuck. Even the most open, vulnerable, risk-taking people need to do this work within a relationship. The benefits are derived from articulating what you're struggling with, how you feel about it, and receiving feedback about the feelings you're expressing.

This relationship dynamic is crucial for making the process effective, and in the next chapter you'll find tools and techniques for building and maintaining relationships.

CHAPTER 8

RELATIONSHIPS: MAKING THE COVERT OVERT

Relationships aren't accidental. It's no coincidence that people in long-term relationships live longer. It's also no coincidence that most people who are highly successful and productive are superior relationship builders. The typical everyday distinctions between relationships like supervisor, colleague, subordinate, client, family member, and friend are not what I'm addressing here. What I'm referring to are the common elements of an ongoing person-to-person interaction that expands both parties' self-knowledge and causes change and growth to come about. These elements are the same regardless of the roles played by the people involved. I've noticed over the years that established, successful people as well as up-and-coming players are the same, whether they're talking to their buddies, their manager, their assistant, or the founder of the company. Without relationships, we would atrophy rather than grow in our personal and professional lives. Yet many of us take them for granted, assuming they're nice additions to our life but not all that essential when compared to "other things." Relationships, however, make other things possible—things like productivity, effectiveness, and success.

You can't grow in isolation. You can't identify your *familiar* and create a new, healthier one on your own. The process requires a relationship, and not just any type of relationship. If it only provides companionship and comfort, it won't do you any good. A dog can keep you company, and a nice chair is comfortable. A growth-oriented relationship is one that challenges you and causes discomfort. Before we look at how to develop this type of relationship, let's start out by clearly distinguishing a growth-oriented relationship from one that invites stagnation.

THE DIFFERENCE: PASSIVE LISTENING VERSUS ACTIVE RESPONDING

At work and at home, many relationships are little more than mutual toleration societies. Think of the unspoken pacts people make at work to allow each other to "get by." A supervisor looks the other way when his subordinate consistently comes in late for work, and the subordinate never confronts his supervisor about the ethical shortcuts he takes to get projects done on time. In a marriage, the wife may tolerate her husband's lack of ambition while the husband tolerates his spouse's obsessive need for security. They mutually tolerate each other because one or both people want a relationship in which "everything I do is accepted." What they don't want is to be judged. To them, a great relationship is having someone who listens but who never argues. "Peaceful coexistence" is a term from an earlier decade that describes what these people want. We need to understand what a good relationship is, as opposed to a mutual toleration society. Specifically, the former is about being judged, having high expectations that keep getting higher, conditional acceptance, commitment to mutual growth, and consistent and constant renewal.

In the sixties, encounter groups and similar movements encouraged people to express their feelings freely but without any accountability. Encounter groups passed from the scene because they failed miserably as personal-growth vehicles. Often people don't understand that they're not going to develop unless someone holds them accountable for taking action based on the feelings they express.

Certainly expression of feelings is important in a growth relationship. It is critical to have freedom to share fears and doubts that we might be uncomfortable sharing outside the relationship. Speaking what's unspoken—making the covert overt—is central to the growth process. Just as important, however, is feedback. Specifically, relationship partners need to provide consistent, honest responses to what we say. Without this feedback, we lapse into an "I'm OK, you're OK" mind-set and continue doing the same things we've always done. This, of course, only gets us what we've always gotten. Feedback eventually leads to new actions, different reactions, and new and better results.

ASSESS CURRENT RELATIONSHIPS

Sometimes it's difficult to know if an existing relationship is helping you to grow. When thinking about it, you may be uncertain about whether you can talk about deep fears or if you can receive honest feedback from a given individual. To help you make that determination, ask yourself the following questions about important relationships in your life:

Do I receive feedback when I share something? Many relationships are nothing more than mutual monologues where one person simply waits for the other person to stop talking so they can start. The conversational dynamic is virtually nonexistent.

Does the feedback relate to what I said? Some people respond to themselves rather than you. Their feedback has little to do with the feelings you expressed and much more to do with their own issues.

Am I putting more into the relationship than I'm getting back? People often stay in relationships far longer than they should or fail to demand more out of them because they have a history with someone. Perhaps they've worked together for years, went to college together, or grew up in the same neighborhood. I know someone who recently went to a college reunion, and he told me that he sat there hearing the same stories that he had heard at other reunions: "I realized I was listening and giving them very honest feedback and they were giving me nothing; I'd grown a lot in the intervening years and they didn't seem to have grown much at all. There no longer was the basis for a relationship." It's important to evaluate the relationship from the perspective of the present rather than the past. Don't take for granted that certain relationships *ought* to exist in your life.

Are you receiving feedback that tells you what to do, or does it take the form of questions? When people tell you what you should do, it usually reflects unhappiness in their lives. Lacking control over their own lives, they feel compelled to control yours. Telling people what to do prompts a defensive response and results in a power struggle; it fails to address the core issue. Let's say you've been in a long-term relationship but can't make a commitment to get married. Your friend says, "You've been going out with her for so long, you ought to marry her." Contrast that "order" with this question: "I'm curious about what you're getting out of this. Where do you see the growth in your relationship with her? Has anything changed in the last seven years?"

Is the relationship always comfortable, or is there a regular and consistent amount of discomfort? Completely comfortable relationships encourage stagnation and mediocrity. When no one challenges you or demands anything from you, you've become an object of neglect or abandonment. You've also been robbed of the most important catalyst for change and growth.

FORMING NEW RELATIONSHIPS

Different people choose different types of relationships. Some form more personal than professional ones; others, vice versa. Some people rely on one relationship with a spouse or a mentor, while others enter (and exit) a series of relationships with work colleagues, friends, and siblings. It doesn't matter what form your relationship takes or how many relationships you have, as long as there's a genuine commitment to growth on the part of both people.

If you're perfectly happy with your life the way it is and have no interest in change, then you should put this book down immediately and forget about creating growth-oriented relationships. If, however, you're experiencing some dissatisfaction and want to change, learn, and develop, then take the initiative to self-disclose before the relationship actually forms.

In other words, share your feelings first. This is a big risk because you have no idea if the person you're talking to will respond positively; he or she might laugh you out of the office. To take this risk, you need to be confident that you'll be able to deal with any type of reaction you receive. When you self-disclose first, you don't need to trust others. Instead, you need to trust yourself sufficiently that you can rebound from rejection, scorn, or any other negative reaction and try again.

What does self-disclosure look like in a relationship? Here are some examples:

To a manager: "I wanted to let you know why I participated so little in our team meetings. You seem to know everything that's going on, and you seem to get everything done without any problems. I've felt so inadequate that I just kept my mouth shut."

To a subordinate: "You need to know that this has been a difficult time for me. The merger and integration of the two companies has just exhausted me; our youngest child leaves for school next month; and our biggest client is acting even more nutty than usual."

To a client: "We've made some hiring mistakes in the last couple of years and you folks have partly paid the price for them. We've realized and confronted this situation and have begun to correct it. We're convinced that our move to upgrade these positions will improve our service to you, but we'll need your patience and understanding through the transition."

To a new friend: "I'm a tough person to have for a friend. My work is superimportant to me and takes up a lot of my time and energy. Nobody gets a whole bunch of my time, but the time they get is really focused and fun. I think I'm worth it, but then again I'm prejudiced."

The other option to self-disclosure—to wait for another person to self-disclose first—isn't viable. Most people aren't willing to take the risk self-disclosure involves, and if you wait for someone to come up to you and start talking about how he really feels, you could be waiting a long time. Most of us, however, do wait for others because we've been burned in relationships before and don't want to get burned again.

One of the great myths in our culture is that relationships only work when we can trust the other person all the time. As important as trust is, it's unrealistic to think no one will ever let you down. Organizations as well as individuals subscribe to this myth. In executive suites, you frequently hear top managers worrying about their lack of total consistency in what they tell employees and their fears that their people no longer trust them. Any organization with the goal of never letting anyone down is doomed to failure.

Similarly, you're never going to form a growth-oriented relationship if you expect the other person to be perfect. We've seen people establish terrific relationships with colleagues only to become disillusioned when they discover the other person is flawed. For instance, they learn their mentor has a drinking problem and think, "I'm sitting here listening to a guy who's an alcoholic! I must have been out of my mind to believe he could help me!" The key question to ask is: *Is this person forthright about his problem and doing something about it?* People are going to disappoint you and violate your trust; that's a given because people aren't perfect. If people only accepted perfection, no parent would hang in there with her child. No spouse would hang in there with a marriage. No employee would hang in there with a company. As long as they take ownership of the problem and attempt to solve it, then they're moving in the right direction. If they consistently violate your trust, of course, that's the wrong direction and indicative of a value mismatch. The point is to not fall into the trap of disillusionment and cynicism. If you do, you're going to avoid relationships and embrace isolation.

VERBALIZING DEMANDS AND EXPECTATIONS

People are often reluctant to articulate what they want from a relationship in its initial stages. They feel as if they're being pushy or asking for too much. Whether it's a personal or a professional relationship, if you don't state your demands and expectations up front, they will become destructive points of contention later on.

When I was getting to know Arleah and realized that this could be a special relationship, I felt obligated to tell her what I expected. I was very direct in telling her that my commitment to my work was very high and this commitment involved a great deal of travel. I also made it clear that I had a certain political outlook that I needed a partner to share and that I never, ever did work around the house—I preferred to make more money and pay others to do that work. What was most important to me, however, was to know that she shared my commitment to trying new things and taking risks. I wanted to determine if Arleah shared my belief that we should never look back at our lives with a sense of regret about not having tried something that challenged and stretched us. I then asked her what her expectations and demands were, and Arleah made them equally clear to me. Among other issues, I accepted her demand that she be in charge of house-related issues, since I wasn't going to be there as much as she was.

When I told Arleah my expectations, I took a big risk—as did she when she told me hers, of course. She could have responded that I was being ridiculous and that the relationship was over. I was willing to accept that consequence, though of course I would have been tremendously sad about it. At the same time, however, I was optimistic about Arleah's need to hear my expectations and articulate her own.

There's no reason you can't do the same thing at work. When you're being recruited, make the following determination of the person who is interested in you: *Is an organization willing to help you grow?*

You can make this determination by making it clear that you don't want to be stuck doing the same thing for years and that you're looking for a job where you're constantly trying new things and receiving fresh challenges. Let's say you have a background in finance and you go in for a job interview. You make it clear that you're looking for a position where you can develop and grow. Here are three possible responses you might receive:

Response No. 1: "Right now we're interested in hiring you for a financial position because that's your background, but we'll watch how fast you learn and how well you do at your job, and if you do well, we're open to moving you onto a track toward any job you want within the organization."

Response No. 2: "This position has been vacant for a long time and we're most concerned about getting someone in here quickly. We're not going to talk about other possibilities, since this is the opening we have and this is what you're interviewing for."

Response No. 3: "We're looking for someone who wants to do this job for the next five or ten years, and if you're looking for job security, this is the place to be."

The first response is indicative of an organization open to nurturing you and meeting your expectations; the odds are that the relationship you form with your supervisor will be a growth-oriented one. It's doubtful that you'll get your expectations met by Response No. 2. The third response is a five-to-ten-year jail sentence in a place where nothing changes and growth is not even a consideration.

Once you begin working at a company, you can test the relationship you have with your manager by confronting him with your desire to grow and tackle assignments beyond your function. You need to take the initiative and ask about the options open to you. When you talk to him about these issues, he might respond as follows:

It's too early to talk about these issues. You just got here; just do what we hired you to do.

A more growth-oriented response would be a series of questions designed to elicit what new things you hope to learn, what kind of assignments interest you, and the direction in which you want your career to go. It's equally important that you hear about the company's future direction and growth and about what their expectations are in order to be a player in their future. A good sign would be if your manager asks you to clarify your expectations by writing them down and talking with you about the next steps that will meet your expectations. You want to obtain specific feedback about what you have to do to be considered for other opportunities.

As you make your expectations clear to your relationship partner (and as your partner makes his expectations clear to you), the relationship will progress only if both people are increasingly willing to self-disclose. As people reveal more about themselves, they are more willing to trust each other and are better able to confront uncomfortable issues. You'll find that when you really open up and talk about how you feel about work and organizational issues, the growth potential of the relationship rises.

REAL-TIME FEEDBACK

One of the hallmarks of growth relationships is that people give each other feedback sooner rather than later. They don't wait hours, days, or weeks to tell the other person how they feel or to challenge them with questions. If something happens at work that is disturbing or disappointing, feedback should follow on the heels of the incident.

For instance, I had just walked into our offices one morning when a longtime colleague approached and greeted me with a broad smile and said, "Your name again? Oh yeah, it's Morrie, Morrie Shechtman, right?" He was clearly taking a shot—albeit a humorous one—at my infrequent visits to our offices. He then launched into a nonstop tale of woe about a report I had sent him from the road that he was having trouble downloading. I was aware of the problem and had asked someone to work on it with his assistant. Still, it was obvious that he wanted to get something done about the report immediately, and he was blaming me for his inability to do so. I felt as if I had run into an emotional buzzsaw; he was making all sorts of assumptions about what had happened that had nothing to do with me.

My initial impulse was to avoid dealing with this issue immediately. All I wanted to do was get to my office, have my tea, and catch up on some work. The last thing I wanted to do was to tell someone whom I valued and respected deeply that I was disappointed in how he approached me. If I had delayed talking to him about this matter—or if I had ignored it completely—the negative feelings produced by this incident would have surfaced at some point in the future. But they would surface in a way that might have nothing to do with what was happening in the present. I might snap at him in a meeting or turn my mind off when he talked. He, of course, would be completely puzzled as to why I was acting this way, and the relationship would suffer as a consequence.

That's why I overcame my initial impulse and gave him feedback a few minutes later, saying: "The way you hit me with a demand as soon as I entered the office made me feel like I had failed you in some way and you were chastising me for it. My first impulse was to make excuses, protect myself, and get as far away from you as possible. I don't like feeling that way, and it certainly doesn't help our relationship." We talked about the incident and about why he acts this way at times. His role in our organization is critically important, and he often is in the thick of the action. This particular week, however, he was atypically uninvolved in the projects that were going on. Because he wasn't particularly busy, he was vulnerable to his *familiar:* having no impact on and little connection with people he valued. Our talk took ten minutes, and this conversation strengthened and reaffirmed our relationship.

Striving for real-time feedback is crucial, especially in work environments where time is precious. When people delay giving each other feedback, they invariably become involved in arguments when they finally confront the issue; too much time has passed to remember the incident clearly, and they become embroiled in debates over the details of what took place. They waste time and energy trying to reconstruct the initial incident, instead of resolving the relationship issues.

Interpersonal efficiency is a significant benefit of real-time feedback. The phrase "cut to the chase" is applicable here. When touchy issues are involved, people will bend over backward to avoid being direct. It's not comfortable to confront someone about a sensitive subject, and it's easy to rationalize how it's better to wait until the situation has cooled down. Waiting will only sidetrack you onto tangential issues, build resentment, and make it more difficult to accomplish important goals quickly. The myth is that "we don't have time for this personal stuff; we've got a business to run." In reality, interpersonal efficiency helps people avoid dancing around tough decisions and lets them address core business concerns quickly.

To give you a sense of how interpersonal efficiency reduces the time necessary to deal with issues, consider how a consultant who trained with us resolved the following problem. We had just finished a series of workshops in San Diego, and only had ten minutes, before we had to leave for the airport and catch a plane. The consultant, Hank, came up to me with another man who had attended Hank's workshop and was galvanized by the experience. Hank explained that the man had approached him and started talking about his twenty-five-year marriage to an alcoholic and how it was damaging his children's lives and his career. Hank wasn't sure how to handle the situation, but rather than put the man off or tell him to schedule an appointment with a therapist, he knew that the man needed real-time feedback. So Hank tracked me down and asked the man to summarize his story. The man did so. I asked him a few very direct questions ("Are you willing to put your twenty-five-year relationship on the line by bringing in an intervention team?"), and told him how to go about locating some resources in his area. I had never met the man before, and I didn't have much time to build a relationship, but he was obviously in pain, ready to listen, and able to focus. I didn't tell him what to do. I helped him take action about his concern, and identify his choices and possible resources.

This was interpersonally efficient. If Hank had not dealt with this man's problem immediately, the emotional impact of the workshop would have worn off and he would have thought of a thousand excuses to avoid addressing the problem.

SELF-DISCLOSURE AND THE *FAMILIAR*

The more you self-disclose, the more you break from your *familiar*. The break usually isn't immediate and dramatic. Typically, most of us begin by disclosing something relatively minor in a relationship, then move on to bigger, more significant things. For instance, we might tell a colleague that "the organization really should address some issues in our area." From there, he might move to a more personal disclosure: "I'm really disappointed in how they haven't let me take on new responsibilities." At some point in the future, this person might have sufficient trust in himself and in the relationship to confess, "These last few weeks have been awful; a minute doesn't pass when I don't think about not only quitting this job, but getting out of this field entirely."

This self-disclosure brings the *familiar* into play. For instance, your *familiar* (and a very common *familiar* for millions of people) might be that when you open up to people, they change the subject because they prefer to hear your thoughts rather than your feelings. So when you tell a colleague that you're disappointed in the company, they may tell you that it's a great place to work and start describing the company's plans for the future.

This is what is familiar: You share your feelings and they get shoved off to the side in favor of a less threatening subject. As a result, you and your colleague enter into a discussion of the organization's five-year plan. Somewhere inside, however, a voice is saying: "What in the world does this have to do with the feelings I just shared?"

If you want to develop a growth relationship, this is the point where you have to break from the *familiar* and say something to the effect of "Well, that corporate vision sounds good, but I'm still very disappointed in how I've been treated. Have you ever felt this way?" If your colleague responds, "How about them Bears?" you know this isn't a relationship worth pursuing.

On the other hand, you might prompt the person to open up about how she was disappointed when she first joined the company and confronted her boss about it; how they had a great talk and her boss made a commitment to help her explore new areas; and how she still sometimes is disappointed but that the company is a place where you don't have to pretend everything's great when it's not and people are generally responsive if you want to learn and grow.

This is the sort of response that helps you break with your *familiar* by validating your feedback and also challenging you. Whether explicitly or implicitly, the challenge in your colleague's response is: Are you just crying "woe is me" or are you taking responsibility for doing something about your situation?

THE PROBLEM WITH RELATIONSHIPS

As you form new relationships, you need to make sure that both you and the other person are growing at roughly the same rate. From the very start of the relationship, this commitment must be there from both of you. If one person is learning and developing at a fast pace and the other person is stagnating, the relationship is going nowhere. While it's difficult to maintain exactly the same pace, you want to avoid big gaps.

Business relationships routinely fall apart because of these gaps; however, marriages offer an even more dramatic example of how divisive these gaps can be. When one spouse spends twenty-five years involved in a high-growth and challenging series of jobs and her partner stagnates in a family business that he was pressured by parents to join, tremendous strain is placed on the marriage. The same strain can be placed on the relationship if one person works outside the home and the other stays home and takes care of the kids. This doesn't mean being a homemaker is automatically a no-growth or low-growth role, any more than working outside the home is automatically a high-growth role. Your particular role doesn't determine the rate or pace of change. It can be challenging and high-growth or boring and stultifying, depending on whether it's done out of a false sense of "duty" or out of a drive for impact and self-discovery.

Another big relationship problem involves one person taking responsibility for both ends of the relationship. Instead of helping a partner grow, you try to make them feel good all the time. You take it upon yourself to cheer them up, to invite them to share in your triumphs, to absolve them of any responsibility to learn, develop, and grow. This caretaking stance is the opposite of real caring, and it often is the result of a caretaking role early in life. This role exhausts the caretaker and makes the recipient feel incapable of accomplishing anything on his own. We see these relationships between supervisors and their employees as well as siblings and spouses.

MUTUAL GOAL-SETTING

Each person brings individual goals to a relationship, and these goals produce creativity and stimulation. Sharing how one hopes to meet challenges and capitalize on opportunities sparks ideas and interest. But a goal must be set for the relationship as well, one that dovetails with individual goals. For instance, one mutual goal for a relationship might be helping each other network effectively so we can succeed in this company.

Both people continually share with each other the realities of organizational life. They talk about opportunities they see emerging, people from whom they can learn and exchange other important information with. Mutual goals give relationships a purpose and guide the interactions.

In our accountability groups, our stated goal is to provide feedback so that people can remove obstacles to their professional success. Everyone understands that they're going to receive tough feedback—that we're going to confront them if they're just being observers or if they're erecting their own obstacles to success. But everyone knows this feedback has a purpose that they've all bought into, making everyone more receptive to challenges and new ideas.

Most people keep their mutual goals covert rather than make them overt. It's scary to articulate these goals. Once you do, you're committed to doing something about them. You have to think about what happens if you achieve the goal and how it might change your life. Verbalizing goals and acting upon them makes them real. If we don't have mutual goals, all we do is walk around unhappy and spend our time complaining about bosses, organizations, and our lives in general.

In 1990, Arleah and I decided we didn't like where we were living and wanted to move. We agreed on the goal of relocating by 1995, and on doing research in the interim to achieve this goal. It was a big risk to broach this subject with Arleah. When I told her, "I don't look forward to coming to this home, it feels awful," she could have misinterpreted my remark and wondered if there was something wrong with her. When I verbalized my feelings, however, Arleah talked about how she felt about where we lived, and it was clear we were both unhappy with the environment. We began doing research about where we might move, and five years later we relocated to Montana.

We had to confront a variety of major issues along the way: How would the move affect our children, how would it impact many members of our family who lived in the Chicago area, what did the move mean in work terms, could we afford it? It wasn't easy, but we made the changes necessary to achieve our mutual goal.

Friends and business associates often ask us how we did it. They say things like "I wish I could do that" and "You people really seem to have achieved your dreams." The way we achieved them is the same way two people in a work relationship achieve their "dreams" of productivity and success: by expressing dissatisfaction or disappointment and creating a mutual goal to change these feelings.

In a work environment, one person may feel he made a terrible mistake going to a company two years ago. If he has a growth relationship, he can verbalize that feeling and create a mutual goal with his partner to find a way out of the company. If this goal isn't set, he'll simply use the relationship to whine and complain about what a miserable employer they have. Mutual goals catalyze change.

They also force us to confront what we value. This is the payoff of growth relationships and what puts us on a developmental path. Do you value the security of having a job, or do you value a career filled with change and exciting new challenges? When you articulate your goal, you put your money where your mouth is. When you've involved another person you care about in setting and achieving a goal, you're putting a lot on the line and you must determine what's really important in your life. This is Internal Frontier territory, and while it can be a risky, scary place, in a growth relationship you're not out there alone.

CHAPTER 9

HOW TO CREATE AN ACCOUNTABILITY GROUP

No matter what type of organization you run or work for, events take place within it that "push back" at who you are. During the course of an average work week, you have to deal with difficult bosses, unhappy subordinates, diverse work teams, challenging goals, sudden crises, and many other scenarios that present opportunities for self-discovery.

Many of us fail to take advantage of these opportunities because we're not aware of what they represent or how we can capitalize on them. People often view the organizational world as a place where self-exploration is forbidden; they believe that they shouldn't bring their personal problems into the office. In fact, it's the perfect environment in which to explore the Internal Frontier. It's an environment that throws people back to their *familiar* faster and more often than almost anywhere else; it's a place where a boss or a colleague is likely to be a symbol and where contrast places are frequently found; and it's a world in which extraordinary opportunities exist for growth and development.

Organizations are ideal places to implement the process of identifying the *familiar* and creating healthier ones. You don't do this work in isolation. While you certainly can implement this process in a relationship of your choosing (at work or in your personal life), often it helps to work within a formal organizational structure. Accountability groups are a structure with which we've had great success in our consulting work for a wide variety of organizations. From professional practices to financial services, high-tech companies to manufacturing plants, people have responded positively to straight talk, unadorned feedback, and the challenge to grow. Job roles and location in the hierarchy have been irrelevant in determining receptivity to the groups.

Each profession and industry has its challenges and its particular defenses against openness and vulnerability. But each also has readily adopted the structure, and in a surprisingly short period of time (i.e., in two or three meetings) experienced high levels of self-disclosure, useful feedback, and efficient resolution of problematic issues. Groups of six to eight people that focus on accelerating learning and growth are excellent environments in which to explore the Internal Frontier. I'd like to share with you what these groups entail, what makes them effective, and how to set them up.

FORMALIZING THE FEEDBACK

Organizations are potential gold mines for feedback, and accountability groups are a great way to help companies realize this potential. Unfortunately, many people fear receiving or giving feedback; they don't want to show others a "weakness" or make someone else uncomfortable. If, however, the right atmosphere is created, people are willing to provide others with clear and compelling feedback.

Dan is a colleague who earlier in his career was running a 500-person division in a midsize company. He figured he was next in line for a position that opened up, and when he went to his boss to talk about that possibility, he was shocked to learn that he wasn't going to get it. Dan's boss told him, "You're a great guy and you're very talented, but you don't have much of an idea how you affect people you work with. There's an invisible book about you, and everyone at this company knows how to read it but you."

After Dan moved past his disappointment at not getting the job, he decided to find out how he was perceived. To do so, he interviewed about forty people he worked with, and he was pleasantly surprised to find that most of them were more than willing to give him feedback. He learned that most of his coworkers viewed him as a high-control, low-trust person. It was eye-opening for Dan to hear fellow employees talk to him about a person he was only vaguely aware of. Based on their feedback, Dan created a plan and a timetable for himself to change; he also shared his plan with others, received feedback on it, and modified the plan accordingly. This plan had a powerful impact on Dan's career, not only helping him achieve greater career success but giving him the impetus and courage to transition to a low-control, high-trust person.

What Dan did intuitively, accountability groups do in a more structured fashion. In these groups, people give and receive feedback, create action plans based on that feedback, and hold group members accountable for implementing their plans. Typically, these groups involve six to ten people who are members of the same functional work group. The group's manager is involved in the group as a sponsor, a participant, and an observer of the group process. In most instances, the groups meet for about two to four hours once a month, and while some have facilitators from outside the group, many are facilitated by people who have received training in the accountability group process.

Still, there's no one way to form and structure these groups, and you should not feel limited by these parameters. You may want to meet more than once a month or form a group with fewer members, for instance. It will be helpful, however, if you stick to the following protocol:

1. Each group member writes down a specific issue that is troubling him or her; without this issue they can't gain admission to the meeting. This issue must relate to a process, a relationship, or an individual's behavior that is currently a blocker to the member's professional performance and achievement of organizational goals. One person's issue might be that his team and the culture are too conservative for his risk-taking ideas; another issue might be an employee's disappointment with how she didn't receive credit for a program that she helped initiate, and that this has happened to her before; a third might be someone's concern that a given supervisor comes down hard on anyone who disagrees with him, and that prevents the group member from correcting his supervisor's errors.

   It doesn't matter if the individuals have personal control over the issue, or if it is primarily in another person's control. What needs to be explored is what choices have been identified, what negative *familiars* are keeping group members from making productive choices, and what plan of action can be implemented to begin the process of creating a new *familiar*.

2. The group decides which issues to deal with; only one or two can be addressed in a two-hour meeting (three or four issues can be addressed in a longer meeting).

3. The issue is briefly presented and the group provides feedback to the presenter; no one is allowed to remain silent.

4. The person who has received the feedback is invited to respond to it.

5. An open discussion of the issue begins.

6. The group and the presenter of the issue determine specific actions for the latter to carry out within a specified period of time and report back to the group at the next meeting.

WHAT TAKES PLACE IN A MEETING (AND IN THE INDIVIDUAL)

What's preventing you from achieving your goals? What's frustrating you and disappointing you within the organization? These are the types of questions that help people formulate the issues they bring to accountability meetings. Issues should be stated succinctly and clearly, and they should relate to the individual rather than a more generalized "we" (i.e., "None of us here are given credit for our ideas").

For instance, a manager named Brenda arrived at an accountability group and described her issue as follows:

I'm very frustrated that everyone acts like my ideas are right, but treats me like I have no influence and usually ignores me.

Brenda described this issue with examples, demonstrating how people didn't really respond to her and how the only way she could get people's attention was to be strident. The feedback she received was across the board, from mystification as to why she lacked influence to a challenge: "Brenda, you are saying this so matter-of-factly and without emotion, I'm not really convinced that this is that important to you." At first Brenda didn't get it. But one example emerged that really helped her drill down to the core issue. The facilitator of the group noted that a while back, Brenda had mentioned that she didn't like the way an incentive plan was being structured. Her offhand manner, however, made it seem as if this was only a minor complaint. Later, after the plan was enacted, she was angry and complained. Obviously, Brenda had strong feelings about the plan, but she failed to assert herself. The group talked to Brenda about other instances where her seemingly accepting and mild manner prevented others from knowing her thoughts about an issue—or how strong her opinions were on a given subject. The fact that five or six people were giving her the same basic feedback made it impossible for her to ignore it.

This unassertiveness was a pattern in Brenda's life, and as she began to explore and identify the repetitive patterns in her past behaviors, she began to define her *familiar*. Her life had been characterized by the people around her anticipating what they believed she needed and providing it before she could articulate or ask for it. Sometimes their definition was accurate, but many times it was not. This situation put Brenda in a real bind. When other people's definitions of Brenda's needs didn't match hers, she found it difficult to voice her dissatisfaction. Since people were trying so hard to meet her needs, communicating that they weren't would only make her look ungrateful and selfish. Ironically, the people who cared most about Brenda were methodically shutting down her ability to ask for what she felt she needed. They were killing her with their idea of kindness.

In the course of this discussion, Brenda realized that she was reproducing this pattern in both her personal and professional lives. She was nice, easy to deal with, had great ideas, and didn't ask for much. So Brenda's *familiar* was that everyone was happy with her except herself.

Brenda needed to take the risk of not being so nice; she needed to be more confrontational and direct when her needs weren't met. Her accountability group assignment was to run another executive's staff meeting in his absence. The first half of the meeting was a disaster. The staff people rolled over her agenda, ignoring her half-hearted attempts to gain control of the meeting and cover the necessary subjects. When the meeting resumed after lunch, Brenda stood up and said, "Enough of this crap! Here's the agenda for the rest of the meeting, we're going to cover all these points. Joe, let's start with you." Throughout the rest of the meeting, Brenda kept everyone in line. Later, when one of my associates asked her how the meeting went, she said, "Terrible." When he asked her why, she said, "Everyone must have thought I was a bitch."

My associate convinced Brenda that it would be worthwhile to ask the attendees what they thought of the meeting. They said that it was a terrific meeting where they "really accomplished a lot" and that Brenda "kept us focused, which is what we needed."

Brenda didn't transform herself overnight. Because change isn't linear, she's going to go back and forth between her old and new behaviors. The accountability group, however, won't let Brenda off the hook. As with any growth relationship, the group confronts Brenda with behaviors that are tied to her *familiar* and gives her the opportunity to talk about her feelings and change her actions.

THREE EXAMPLES: ACCOUNTABILITY GROUPS IN ACTION

Accountability groups deal with a wide variety of personal development issues that directly impact professional performance. Here are three brief examples of the impact they can have on organizational performance:

1. A senior-level human resources executive had a key role identifying management talent for a high-growth telecommunications company. In his accountability group, however, he was consistently quiet and almost withdrawn. He had a wealth of experience in high-growth cultures, but few were benefiting from his knowledge and skills. His passivity and lack of involvement in the group were confronted, and what emerged was a long history of having his input ignored or discarded and equally deep feelings of hurt at being routinely discounted.

This feeling of having something to offer and not having it accepted was his familiar. *This familiar was intimately tied to his distant and superficial relationship with his father, whose health was steadily declining. Part of the action plan that came out of his accountability group was to work on his relationship with his father and try to establish a meaningful connection with him before the father died. He worked on this during a number of visits to his father's home, and the results were remarkable. He shared feelings with his father that he never had before, and he felt a real connection with him before his father's death.*

During this time, he became an active participant in the accountability group, and has been vocal and instrumental in the growth of other group members. He also has become a key player in the operational performance of the company by challenging practices and behaviors that he had previously ignored.

2. An accountability group comprised of administrative assistants had a knotty issue to deal with. They all worked in close physical proximity to each other, and all had very good working relationships with their bosses. One of them, however, didn't get along with the others and didn't have much respect for them.

The group struggled to confront this person. They finally surfaced their feelings about her curtness and abruptness, her extreme moodiness, and her rudeness with some clients. She soon shared her feelings that she resented being grouped together with the other "admins" since she felt that her role for her boss was very special and different from anything done by her colleagues.

Her familiar *was feeling alone in the midst of people and not knowing how to connect with them. The need to always be special was a convenient cover for her familiar sense of sadness and isolation. Her action plan involved taking a huge risk: doing things just like her colleagues did and being like them. This meant giving up her long-standing special status and beginning to grieve her lack of closeness with key figures in her life. As she did this, her counterproductive work behaviors dramatically diminished and the productivity of the whole group increased.*

3. An experienced and formerly very successful sales professional had reached a critical juncture in his career. His prospecting activity was minimal, his results were flat and getting flatter, and his financial situation was steadily declining. In presenting his issue to his accountability group, he received some unanimous and sobering feedback. Everyone in the group found him to be uninspiring and boring. If they found him that way, there was a good chance that his prospects and customers harbored similar feelings. He got additional feedback that the boredom he created kept people at a distance. He might as well have been wearing a sign: "Stay away from me, I'm uninteresting and awfully boring." His familiar *was desperately wanting help from others and getting silently rebuffed.*

What emerged from his interactions in the group was the goallessness of his life, his need for help in formulating new goals, and his quiet panic that no one would ever be interested in befriending and helping him. One of his action plans was to identify a colleague, establish a growth and accountability relationship that would confront his worst fears, and help him reset a direction for his life. He did this and embarked on a new success track that not only benefited him but also helped his sales associates (many of whom were struggling with their own goallessness) and the overall company results.

FACILITATING GROUPS

We've found that certain actions help and others hinder accountability groups. The following facilitating tips will help you avoid mistakes and increase a group's efficacy.

Don't run from strong emotions and intense interactions. Nothing diminishes the effectiveness of an accountability group faster than avoiding confrontation. We incorrectly assume that others are fragile; we're convinced that a negative word or direct criticism will cause them to fall to pieces. Our caretaking mentality makes us intent on keeping others happy. In reality, people are far stronger than we assume. We all have tremendous resilience and a great capacity to absorb and use criticism.

In accountability groups, feelings often become intense. When this happens, people tend to back off. They tell a joke, switch the subject, or do anything else that will diminish the intensity of the emotion being expressed. One of the most common ways of deflecting emotion is by intellectualizing it. In other words, someone responds to the emotion of the moment by saying, "Let me tell you what's really going on here. Jane is upset because there aren't enough women in authority around here. . . ." In reality, Jane is furious and totally fed up with her coworkers who sit in the same room and consistently patronize her, ignore her input, and solicit feedback from others who have half Jane's intelligence and insight. She's also disgusted with herself for letting this happen and not confronting it. These intellectual red herrings send people onto "safer" ground; no one has to risk exposing his feelings when issues are intellectualized. Most people who do this are responding to their own fears and discomfort rather than out of concern for the person who is expressing strong feelings. While it's important to avoid hostile exchanges (hostility also diverts people from expressing and exploring their deep-level feelings), intensity and discomfort are catalysts for identifying the *familiar*.

Move discussions to a deeper level. People frequently cling to surface issues, avoiding the deeper emotions that take some effort and risk to reach. For instance, we worked with a manager who had developed an innovative pricing model that the sales department was ignoring. In the accountability group, he exhibited typical victim behavior: complaining about the sales department, saying that no one cared about all his hard work, whining that he had wasted a great deal of his time designing this model. One of the questions we asked him during the feedback session was: "Have you confronted the head of sales about this problem?" He had not. His assignment at the end of this meeting was to do so. When we met again the next month, this manager told the group he still hadn't been able to get together with the sales director, claiming that they couldn't coordinate their schedules.

If the group had stopped there—if they had simply discussed his inability to confront senior executives and the irrational fears he had about what they might do if he did confront them—they would have only addressed the surface issue. To their credit, the group probed deeper, asking him what was familiar about the feelings he was experiencing in his current situation. He eventually admitted that he had great difficulty confronting any woman in authority; he also related that when he was a child he was deathly afraid of contradicting or challenging his mother, knowing that if he did there would be a high price to pay—a price fraught with guilt and angst for giving this self-sacrificing, kind, and fragile person such a hard time.

Accountability groups drill down the same way people in one-on-one relationships do: by asking questions that prompt individuals to explore their Internal Frontiers (rather than sail "unfeelingly" across the surface of their worlds). For example, Jack is a consultant in charge of coaching the CEO of a large organization. Jack has worked closely with us for years and is aware of his internal issues, but he still reproduces his *familiar* on occasion. This CEO is particularly adept at triggering Jack by accusing him of "not doing things right"—not doing things the way the CEO would do them. Jack's immediate reaction is to want to say "screw you" and quit. Furious and frustrated with this CEO, Jack shared his impulse to quit with his accountability group. The group's feedback helped Jack understand that his reaction was far beyond what the situation called for. Further questions helped him see that the *familiar* feeling he was producing was the disappointment of getting close to someone and then being dumped. Growing up, Jack repeatedly failed to get his father to demonstrate that he cared about him. After a while, Jack washed his hands of the relationship and tried to protect himself from future hurt by determining that he wanted nothing to do with him. The CEO, as a symbol for Jack's father, sends him confusing but familiar messages. On the one hand, he validates Jack and seems to open the door to a relationship by praising Jack for helping him turn the company in a new direction. On the other hand, he picks at the details of Jack's work, leaving him feeling that he can never do anything right. Consequently, Jack finds himself wanting to quit the CEO just as he quit trying to have a relationship with his father.

It was scary for Jack to drill down to this level. As difficult as it was to admit that he messed up a work assignment in front of his peers, it was even more difficult to talk about how this problem made him feel. It was also tough to absorb the group feedback after he took the risk and revealed how he felt. Making yourself vulnerable isn't easy in the relative privacy of a one-on-one relationship, and it's even more difficult in the public arena of an accountability group. Given this difficulty, groups need to facilitate risk-taking by asking questions rather than telling people what to do, and they must resist the temptation to turn the group into a trial or a brainwashing session. The goal of the accountability group is to help expand members' self-knowledge and provide them with viable action plans, not to extract confessions and testimonials or produce miraculous conversions.

Let people know resistance has consequences. People will resist the process. Some will find it difficult to be open and honest. Others won't take the groups seriously. If this happens, it can damage the group dynamic and make it impossible to hold others accountable. We've instituted a series of negative sanctions that have been quite effective. If people arrive at a group meeting without a meaningful issue written out, they're asked to let the group know, take a break, and not return until they've completed this assignment. If they fail to have the issue a second time, they're barred from the meeting. If it happens a third time, it earns them a negative mark in their performance review and might result in termination.

Direct and insistent feedback is another way to communicate that resistance is unacceptable. At one meeting, a participant refused to say anything, demonstrating his disdain with a sardonic smile. Finally another participant said, "I don't understand your attitude. Sam is upset, we're talking about very serious issues, and all you're doing is sitting there grinning." The grinning participant protested that he really did take the meeting seriously. At the next meeting, however, he repeated this behavior. Continued challenges of this kind surfaced other work problems, all connected to this person's cynicism and bitterness. It was clear his attitude inhibited his ability to build relationships with colleagues. A month later, he was fired—not simply because of his resistance in the meeting, but because of his resistance to change in all aspects of his work.

Use the meetings to focus on work done between meetings. In other words, make sure people test new behaviors in the workplace and carry out assignments from the meetings. The idea is for people to bring the results of their risk-taking and new approaches back to the group. At one meeting, a manager noted how he had fulfilled his assignment of confronting his boss about an issue and was chewed out as a result. The group asked him a number of questions: What did you say? What prompted you to confront him? What else was going on at the time? How did you phrase what you said? These questions are critical, helping everyone explore what went wrong and what went right and how people felt about it.

Facilitate using common sense. People often are aghast at the thought of discussing interpersonal issues without a trained therapist to lead the discussion. Perhaps this would be necessary if groups were dealing with truly bizarre behaviors and deeply dysfunctional individuals. In the vast majority of cases, however, the problems people have are not rooted in some major childhood trauma or organic brain damage. Just becoming aware of the problems, talking about feelings, and risking new behaviors goes a long way toward resolving them.

While it helps having a facilitator who has run account-ability groups before, participants are usually able to handle the meetings themselves, though they may need some training and practice. If someone in a meeting says he's happy but he seems to be on the verge of tears when he talks about his work situation, common sense dictates that there's a disconnection; it should cause a group member to ask: "You say you're happy here, but you seem very upset when you talk about your role in the company. What's going on?"

BENEFITS ON MANY LEVELS

An accountability group's impact isn't limited to the person whose issue is being discussed at a particular meeting. Feedback and discussion help everyone work on their own issues and take risks in revealing things about themselves. When someone articulates his problems with taking on authority figures and relates it to his past experiences, others in the group can feel a resonance to similar experiences; they start thinking and talking about how their own personal history has impacted their problems with authority figures. Groups give everyone a chance to share their feelings and grapple with their issues; they learn a new way of communicating and relating to other people.

Another benefit of these groups is that they foster intimacy, vulnerability, and trust among people who work together. The intense interpersonal environment leads to relationships outside of the groups, which helps people grow and develop. Individuals who may have never even considered revealing aspects of themselves to a colleague find themselves much more willing to do so after being together in an accountability group.

Accountability groups are also great testing grounds for leaders. We've seen organizations use these groups as informal selection systems. In every group, there are usually one or two people who take the most risks in revealing their feelings, ask the best questions, and provide direct, insightful feedback. While these behaviors may not have qualified them for leadership positions in the past, they definitely qualify them for leadership roles now and in the future.

Ultimately, however, accountability is the operative word. Groups hold members accountable and expect them to take the risks necessary to change and grow, and, most importantly, to tie this growth to achievement of organizational objectives. This added leverage of needing to achieve results is what distinguishes accountability groups from "simple support groups" and gives them their real power and impact. More than anything else, accountability is what makes these groups viable tools for people who want to break through to a new, more effective level of performance.

CHAPTER 10

PLANNING WHERE YOU'RE GOING TO GROW

Knowing who you are is only part of the process. You also need to know where you're going. Here you're going to discover how to formulate a vision, mission, goals, and values in a way that directs both your personal and your professional growth. You'll discover how to revitalize these tired old concepts by connecting them to who you are as a person. Most goal statements are of the cookie-cutter variety: "I want to be a partner or a senior vice president in ten years." Values are often knee-jerk reactions to political correctness: "I value diversity." Personalizing and internalizing these concepts will help you explore the Internal Frontier with greater confidence.

Another error this chapter will correct is that vision, mission, goals, and values are generally formulated from a professional perspective. It's assumed that you can experience tremendous growth at work and in your career but still remain a slug in your personal life. Professional and personal growth are inextricably linked, and to try to focus on one at the expense of the other dooms your efforts in both.

As you explore the Internal Frontier, you're going to start growing. How are you going to direct this growth? As you stop reproducing your *familiar* and create a new, healthier one, you're going to be much more effective and productive. The purpose of having a vision, mission, goals, and values is to capitalize on this increased effectiveness and productivity. Let's examine how you can create a create a growth plan and use it personally and professionally.

VISION: DEFINING A PREFERRED FUTURE

A vision is a clear, concise, idealized picture of a preferred future. It's optimistic and hopeful, the deepest expression of what we want. It should be composed in the form of a direct statement, one that's inspiring and in keeping with your beliefs. Here are three examples:

> *"I want to demystify the human process."*
> *"I will have a tremendous, positive impact on everyone I meet and work with."*
> *"I am going to make a contribution in my field that will make the world a better place to live in."*

These vision statements are memorable and motivating. They point people in a direction and guide them if they happen to get lost or stuck along the way. They are also very difficult, if not impossible, to achieve. This paradox makes sense when you realize that the point of a vision is direction rather than destination. Goals, which I'll discuss a little bit later, provide you with reachable destinations. Your vision pulls you around obstacles and helps you to grow and develop. When you're feeling frustrated and uncertain and don't know if you can continue your work, your vision inspires you and keeps you going. Let's say your vision is the first one I listed, and you're a therapist who has had great difficulty with a number of your patients; they just don't seem to be making much progress despite your best efforts. Perhaps you should take a break from your work. Maybe you should not invest so much of yourself in it. As these thoughts course through your head, you remember your vision: to demystify the human process. You probably will never totally achieve this vision, but it's such a compelling concept that it reenergizes you and reminds you what all your hard work is about. Ultimately, you may only demystify one aspect of the human process for a relatively small number of people, but that's a highly significant accomplishment, and you wouldn't achieve even that if you lacked a larger vision.

Visions catalyze change and growth. To be motivating and effective, they need to address the creation of choices and the delivery of impact on the lives of others. They also give you a sense of "what's in it for you," and help you deal with the risk and pain a vision demands. It's important to understand that creating this vision of a preferred future is painful to do even if you're out there on the Internal Frontier, and impossible to do effectively if you haven't done any self-discovery and are locked into your *familiar*. There's a great deal of loss associated with even thinking about your vision. Articulating it makes this loss even more impactful.

To understand this notion of loss, let me tell you what happens when I ask someone to describe their dreams, which are second cousins to visions. At first they'll laugh awkwardly and protest that dreams are for kids or young idealists. "It's unrealistic to take dreams seriously," they'll explain. What they really mean is that if they talk about their dreams, they might have to do something about them. Arleah and I talked about our dream of moving to Montana, and this was very scary for a number of reasons. By making the dream a real possibility, we had to confront the losses that would occur if we actually moved to Montana: We'd have to leave behind friends and relatives in the Chicago area, we might lose certain clients in the area, and so on.

On a deeper level, we would have to break from that familiar feeling of dreams being nothing more than pipe dreams. For instance: We didn't deserve such a great house in such a beautiful part of the country. Both Arleah and I certainly received this type of message growing up. The move was also scary because we might fail. What if we planned to move and it didn't work out for some reason? In fact, that's what almost happened. For two years after we decided to move, we couldn't secure the financing necessary to build the home we wanted. It was frustrating to think that we might have to stay in a community that we'd already said good-bye to emotionally.

Oscar Wilde said there are two human tragedies: The first is not getting what you want; the other is getting it. That's what is scary about articulating both your dreams and your vision. A vision, however, is rarely achievable. If you're not in touch with your internal issues, you'll find yourself reacting to any vision you create with bitterness and cynicism. As you attempt and fail to make progress in a given direction, you'll blame external forces for your failure. That's why it's crucial to identify your *familiar* and work on creating a healthier one. People who do so are optimistic and confident; they're able to pursue their vision with great resilience. When they go off track, they don't start blaming people and things for their problems. Because they know who they are, they're able to marshal the inner strength necessary to get back on track.

It's important to be aware that an unconscious fear of loss may prevent you from crafting a vision. At the same time, there are two other obstacles that might stand in your way:

Perfectionism. People sometimes try too hard when working on their vision statements. They want the statement to be etched in stone, and that's neither necessary nor appropriate. As you mature and grow, your vision may evolve. Right now, it doesn't have to cover all contingencies and possibilities. Commit yourself to putting down on paper an imperfect but inspiring statement about your preferred future.

Friends, loved ones, colleagues. People you know who have plateaued, who are out of touch with their feelings, and who have chosen a no-growth or slow-growth life will do everything possible to discourage your vision. Some of them will respond cynically: "You're never going to have a big impact on anyone in that field." Others will discourage you with a caretaking sentiment: "I just don't want you to be disappointed." What both comments really mean is that they don't want you to leave them behind. If you move in the direction of your vision, *you will* leave them behind. If you grow and reach new levels of success, you'll endanger the relationship. As I've stated earlier, unequal rates of growth do doom relationships. Managers often communicate indirectly that they don't want their people to change; they nitpick and find fault in order to discourage their growth and willingness to try new things.

VISION EXERCISE

Use the following questions and activities to create a personal vision statement. Remember, you don't have to produce the perfect statement. People who haven't done that much Internal Frontier work often end up with statements that reproduce the *familiar*. Others focus simply on materialistic visions—"I want to be one of the richest entrepreneurs in the country." Whatever vision you articulate, think of it as a beginning rather than as a definitive, final statement.

1. What occurrences and/or accomplishments from your past give you great pride today?
   For each, why do you feel as you do?
2. Who are the people in your past whom you impacted?
   For each, what difference did you make and how do you feel about it today?
3. Who are the people whom you impact today?
   For each, how are you making a difference and how does it make you feel?
4. Describe the ideal future.
   How does it compare to today?
   How are you impacting others?
   How will you feel when this ideal future becomes the past?

5. Given your current thoughts and feelings, write a "draft" statement of your vision.

MISSION: THE MAP THAT WILL LEAD YOU TOWARD YOUR VISION

If vision offers an ideal destination, mission provides a kind of map. It gives you a sense of how you'll move toward your vision. It doesn't do so by listing all the possible scenarios and detailing that you'll do y if x occurs. Again, this is a simple statement that will guide your growth. It's an affirmation of sorts, such as:

"I will live a life of openness and honesty."
"I am committed to relationships of reciprocity."
"I am going to pursue new, challenging experiences and be open to change."

Like your vision statement, the mission statement is scary and risky. Remember, this is not just an external affirmation, but an internal one. It means you're making a commitment to pursue your vision in a way that leads you away from the *familiar*. If you've been involved in caretaking relationships most of your life and now you're affirming that you're only going to engage in reciprocal relationships, this affirmation will naturally cause some discomfort. It's also something that people with whom you form relationships will hold you to. When you share your vision and mission statements with others, the latter is what they'll use to keep you accountable. If your relationship partner—someone you can be open and vulnerable with and with whom mutual accountability is a relationship cornerstone—observes you acting paternalistically to a subordinate, he'll call you on it: "You know, your comment to Sam that you'd always support him no matter what seems at odds with your mission statement."

MISSION EXERCISE

1. Who are the most influential people in your life?
   For each person, describe how he influenced you, the qualities you admire most in him, and the qualities you possess that he influenced.
2. As you think about your relationships and roles (family, personal, professional, social, and community), write a brief statement that you would like to have each person make about you.
3. Using your answers to No. 2, outline the necessary activities, behaviors, and beliefs for a successful journey toward your ideal future (as you created it in the previous exercise).
4. Write a brief mission statement based on your responses to this exercise. Be clear, concise, and affirmative.
5. Describe how your mission will move you toward your vision. In describing how it will do so, think about whether it causes you discomfort. How does it move you away from your old *familiar*?

VALUES: DECISION-MAKING MECHANISMS

As you learn and grow and move toward your vision, you'll be faced with a constant stream of decisions, some of which will be difficult and confusing. As you define your values, your choices will be clearer. For instance, let's say your vision involves achieving great leadership and impact. One day someone presents you with an opportunity to run a powerful organization that has built an empire around exploiting sensationalism and shallowness. The clarity of your values will help you decide if the nature of this opportunity fits your definition of leadership and impact.

Values also help you decide how to work on a relationship or whether to continue to develop particular relationships—a relationship with a spouse, a colleague, or a company. When your values feel in sync, but you feel unconnected to a partner, you may need to uncover and work through old *familiars* that have created obstacles to communication. When your values feel fundamentally in conflict, it may be time to face the painful reality that the relationship has come to an end. If an organization values maintaining the status quo over growth (and you value growth), then there's a clear value conflict. If you're struggling with whether you should remain in a comfortable job or leave to find a more challenging one, look to your values.

Whatever values you believe in, they must be unambiguous or else they're not values. To be unambiguous, they must be stated in a manner in which no further questions are needed to clarify their meaning. If further questions can be asked, then they're probably not values. Family, for instance, is often articulated by people as a value. But it fails the test of ambiguity and begs for a series of questions to be asked. Whose family? How do you define a family? From whose perspective? The general notion of "having a close-knit family" may be admirable, but to get to the underlying values, a lot more drilling down is required. We may find that what one person means by "family" is a commitment to everyone's individual growth. What another person means is a commitment to self-sacrifice and preservation of the group. It's important to emphasize that values tell you how to get where you're going.

It's impossible to talk about values in a vacuum. In fact, one of the problems with many individual and corporate statements of values is that they have no context and therefore no meaning to anyone reading them. Since values are measured by action and not intention, they have little or no substance until you *do* something. So talking about values without knowing your goals would be like having a terrific road map with nowhere to go. A number of commonly expressed values such as responsibility, commitment, choice, impact, and honesty only come alive when decisions need to be made in order to achieve a specific set of goals. If, for example, one of your goals is to have a family in which everyone's highest potential is achieved, you can go about doing this in many different ways. If one of your core values is taking care of others, you can create a family system where a comfortable path to achievement is clearly laid out for each member. If, on the contrary, your core value is individual responsibility, you will create a family system in which each person is regularly confronted with choices and decisions and learns that there are consequences for each option chosen. Your values only come into play once you've declared what you want to accomplish.

VALUES EXERCISE

People sometimes have difficulty defining what their values really are. Here's an exercise to facilitate this process:

1. *List what you feel your values are and apply the ambiguity test to them.* True values are unambiguous. One of the best ways to see if your values hold true is to share them with at least two other people who will give you direct feedback. If, for example, you consider "relationships" a value, you may quickly find out that as few as two other people define relationships in very different ways. These differing definitions may then point you in the direction of a true, unambiguous value.

2. *Take your list and describe how you live your values.* If you say one of your values is honesty, how does that manifest itself in your personal and professional life? Do you promise people that you'll be at certain meetings and fail to show up? Do you tell people you'll call them and never do? To avoid telling people hard truths (i.e., they'll be fired if they can't improve their performance), are you deliberately ambiguous and unclear? Put your values to the test by asking these types of questions.

3. *Identify a situation where you made a tough decision based on a specific value.* The idea here is to determine if you've misidentified your values. For instance, someone might say, "My value is stability, and I decided to change jobs because my former employer asked me to travel too much, which took time away from my family, community, and church." How did the notion of stability help this person make the decision to quit? Obviously, it wasn't stability that made him quit, but the real, underlying value of commitment. This person made a commitment

to his family members, community, and church
to be available for a reasonable amount of time
each week.

4. *What were the three most difficult choices you've
had to make thus far in your life?* What values
most determined your decision-making
process?

5. *Think about what a possible value has cost you.*
A real value has consequences. If your value is
honesty, what has it cost you to be honest?
Have you risked being disliked by giving others
honest feedback? Have you ever left a job
because you found your employer unethical in
the way he dealt with customers and you
refused to tolerate it?

6. *Decide which price you prefer to pay.* In other
words, would you rather lose a job because you
upheld your value or would you rather feel
guilty and remorseful (and remain employed)
because you violated it? Either choice comes
with a painful price. If you've effectively identified your values—you've discovered the beliefs
you're willing to live by and act on—the price
is a lot easier to pay, and it always helps move
you toward your goals.

7. *List your five strongest values and again apply the
ambiguity test to them.*

GOALS: MEASURABLE STEPS LEADING
TOWARD YOUR VISION

Goals, unlike visions, are achievable. There's been a great
deal written about goal-setting, and I'm not going to
dwell on this tool. It's important to use primarily when

you're anxious and lost; you're worried—perhaps justifi-ably—that you're doing the wrong things and not head-ing toward your vision. Setting goals is a way of creating signposts along the way; when you reach them, you know you're making progress in the right direction.

The key to creating goals has to do with levels of importance and clarity, as the diagram below makes clear.

The clearer and more important goals are, the greater chance you have of achieving them. For instance, if your goal is "to make a lot of money," that's not very clear. If the importance is that "It would be nice to have more money," that's not particularly significant. If, how-ever, your goal is to save $10,000 this year to begin a

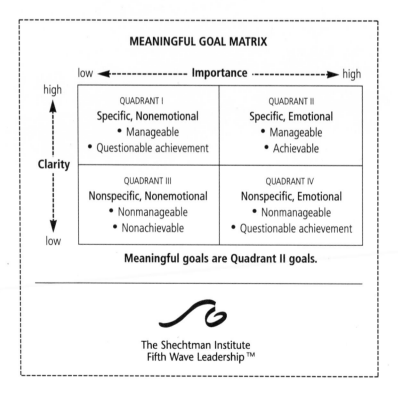

MEANINGFUL GOAL MATRIX

low ◄-------------- **Importance** --------------► high

	QUADRANT I Specific, Nonemotional • Manageable • Questionable achievement	QUADRANT II Specific, Emotional • Manageable • Achievable

high ▲

Clarity

low ▼

	QUADRANT III Nonspecific, Nonemotional • Nonmanageable • Nonachievable	QUADRANT IV Nonspecific, Emotional • Nonmanageable • Questionable achievement

Meaningful goals are Quadrant II goals.

The Shechtman Institute
Fifth Wave Leadership ™

home-based, part-time job or to raise $300,000 in the next year in order to finance a new business venture, then you have increased the odds for success.

Resetting goals is also crucial. You will stop your growth and development dead in its tracks if you set one goal, achieve it, and rest on your achievement. It doesn't matter if the goal is common and widely shared or unusual and lofty, or if you own a home, educate your children, become a partner in a major law firm, are named CEO, or win a prestigious award. Once you achieve your goal, you'll find yourself like kids often do after opening their presents on Christmas day: Is this all there is?

You're most likely to fail after you succeed. Once people achieve a goal and celebrate, they often become listless and sad. As I've illustrated earlier, success entails loss, and it needs to be grieved. If it's not, people will be stuck where they are and lack the impetus to reset their goals. Resetting goals helps spur change and growth. It also helps you keep up with your vision, which will evolve over time.

When you achieve a goal, you're absolutely convinced that this is the highest achievement possible, a crowning glory. In reality, it's simply the joy and pride of the moment. This absolutely deserves to be celebrated. What we need to keep in mind is that this achievement is the signpost on the road to our vision. When we built our home in the Chicago suburbs and had just moved in, we felt like we were living a dream. We were convinced that we would spend the rest of our lives in this beautiful home. Within six months, we were already contem-plating what we'd do differently the next time we built a house.

GOAL EXERCISE

1. Create a list of goals that relate to your vision and mission statements; make sure the goals are clear and important.
2. Create an action plan to help yourself achieve these goals; include specific steps to take and due dates to ensure accountability. Make sure that the action plan is run through your value screen, and that each specific step you're going to take is consistent with your values and consistent with all the other steps in your action plan.
3. Once you achieve these goals, do this exercise again in order to reset them.

OVERCOMING THE OBSTACLES

You're not going to change and grow unless you realize emotionally (as opposed to intellectually) that the gains outweigh the losses. Without a vision, mission, values, and goals, it's difficult to know what that gain will be. When you break from the *familiar* by confronting a boss, making a risky career move, or closing a sale beyond your wildest expectations, you're going to experience loss. The anticipated discomfort of that loss may prevent you from making the change unless you understand the future gain. With your vision articulated and your other tools in hand, you'll be better able to change and grow.

Having the ingredients of a growth plan—the vision, mission, values, and goals—provides you with a tremendous amount of confidence and resiliency. In a highly unpredictable and uncertain world, this plan offers internal security (as opposed to external security, which is fading fast). Marcia was a project manager who had created her own growth plan. She was highly skilled, well-paid, and worked for a market leader. But after formulating her plan and talking about it with a colleague, she realized she was never going to move in the direction of her vision as long as she worked for her current employer. She wanted to have impact on a wide range of people, and that was impossible where she worked. The organization had pigeonholed her as a project manager and didn't want to lose her talent in that area by moving her to a more impactful role. When Marcia decided to quit and look for another job, her friends and family told her she was nuts; they insisted that she had a job others would love to have. Marcia, though, recognized that it was a dead end, and her growth plan gave her the confidence and flexibility to leave her job, change, and pursue her mission and vision.

It's also important to share your vision. You need to use these tools within a growth-focused relationship: a colleague, supervisor, sibling, or spouse. Sharing your vision, mission, values, and goals with someone who will hold you accountable is critical. They can give you feedback you will use to reset goals and reshape your vision.

Perhaps the biggest obstacle to doing the exercises in this chapter, however, is getting started. Typically, people offer the following kinds of excuses as to why they haven't set their vision down on paper: "I'm too busy." "I need more work experience before I do it." "I'm too old for this to matter much in my career." As you might suspect, the real obstacle is internal. There's something inside that's preventing you from going after your dream, and it's valuable to make this discovery as you struggle with these exercises. If you're having problems with them, it's probably because articulating a vision is unfamiliar. You may have grown up in an environment where your dreams were devalued and no one took your ideas seriously.

If this is the case, acknowledge it and be aware of the issues involved. Make a commitment to try these exercises, and don't be concerned if your vision doesn't come flowing out the first time you try to express it. Set a time and place with someone to start working on it. If you want to create a growth plan that encompasses personal as well as professional issues, you must be willing to make this commitment.

PROFILES

PEOPLE WHO HAVE MADE PROFESSIONAL BREAKTHROUGHS THROUGH PERSONAL TRANSFORMATION

CHAPTER 11

DENISE: FROM PLEASER TO PERFORMER

Nothing illustrates the impact of personal transformation on professional growth better than the stories of people who have transformed themselves. I'd like to share the stories of three people who attribute a significant amount of their professional success to this self-discovery process. These are three individuals who have identified their old *familiars* and have taken significant steps in creating new, healthier ones. Though all of them occasionally fall back into old patterns and unproductive behaviors, they have made dramatic progress personally and professionally.

I'm using pseudonyms for each person, not because they're uncomfortable with the public telling of their stories, but because they involve other people—family members and colleagues—who might be uncomfortable. I've also changed company and industry names and taken some license in describing certain incidents in order to maintain their anonymity. What I have not changed are the deeply personal feelings of the three people and how addressing and expressing these feelings impacted their lives.

The three people profiled here are a diverse group: the head of a financial services company's top office, a vice president of a midsize technology company, and an insurance agent. Intuitively and through their work with myself and my colleagues, each identified "defining moments" where they confronted challenging personal issues from their past that catalyzed professional breakthroughs.

In earlier chapters, we've seen brief examples of others who have dealt with these issues and explored the Internal Frontier. The longer, more detailed stories here will give you a better understanding of how to use the process I've described to achieve similar breakthroughs. They capture the drama and pain of confronting these issues and demonstrate how resilient and capable people are of dealing with them and pursuing growth paths.

The profiles are divided into the following six sections:

1. *Professional history*—a synopsis of the individual's career from the past to the present.
2. *Personal history*—a summary of his or her personal life, from childhood to the present.
3. *Legacy*—the skills and baggage each person derived from his or her history.
4. *Internal awareness*—how an individual's self-discovery began; early steps in identifying the *familiar*.
5. *Linkages*—the connection between dealing with personal issues and achieving increased professional success.
6. *Using the process*—how the formal Internal Frontier process facilitates the profiled person's continued growth and change.

As you'll see, each of these people is very different in terms of personality, working style, background, and what's familiar. The similarity is how each one of them carried around an unspoken truth for years, and when they finally found ways to express this truth, they experienced tremendous leaps in productivity, success, and satisfaction.

PROFESSIONAL HISTORY

Denise, age 38, has worked her way up from being a store clerk to her current position of significant responsibility and financial rewards. She has achieved this success despite a lack of advanced degrees and connections; she has come a long way from selling clothes, perfume, and other products in retail chains.

As a regional vice president of operations for a technology company, Denise has six people reporting directly to her and is indirectly responsible for 2,000 employees. She makes $115,000 annually plus a forty percent bonus and has been in her current position for a year. Prior to that, she had another operations job with the same employer, though she supervised a smaller number of people and had less responsibility. Denise has worked for other companies in operations management positions (though they were significantly less challenging than her current position), and she started her career as a retail salesperson. Though she graduated eighth in her high school class, she wasn't particularly interested in college—she attended college for a while but dropped out because she found it "boring." She was anxious to be in the work world, and in fact started working when she was sixteen, balancing a full-time job with school.

In her current job, Denise has to draw on a range of management and customer service skills when dealing with an extremely difficult client. Because it is one of her company's biggest clients, Denise plays a critical role. A number of this company's people are outrageously demanding and verbally abusive, and managers who have been in Denise's position before her have complained bitterly about the "impossible" demands placed upon them. One of their client contacts has been known to jump on tables and scream obscenities when he feels things aren't going right. Even when Denise's company delivers solid results, the client finds something to criticize.

Nonetheless, Denise has earned kudos from management for her adroit handling of these situations. Though the client is never going to change the way it does business with its suppliers, it has a far better relationship with Denise than with any of her predecessors. Denise's ability to build strong, reciprocal relationships has not only made her great at her current job, but it has also given her a highly marketable skill.

PERSONAL HISTORY

Born in the southeastern U.S. in 1960 to a father who was in the military and a mother who was a homemaker, Denise and her sister and two brothers moved constantly because of her father's occupation. She attended thirteen different schools in twelve years. Her father was catered to when he came home from military assignments, and he ordered his wife and Denise and her siblings around as if they were in his command. Denise's mom never challenged her dad, even after he left the military at a relatively young age and worked at a number of jobs (e.g., selling cars, building maintenance). It didn't strike Denise that her parents' marriage was a particularly happy one, and she often found herself trying (ineffectually, in most instances) to "fix" what was wrong with it.

Denise first married when she was very young, and she noted that it resembled her parents' marriage—it was a partnership marked by low expectations and total acceptance. Whatever Denise did was fine with her husband, and he had no ambitions. Her second marriage was to an abusive, critical man who routinely resorted to intimidating tactics to make his point or get his way. Right before the marriage ended, they were having trouble with their dog digging up an earlier pet they had buried in their backyard. One day, her husband took the dog out in the woods and Denise heard a gunshot. Her husband returned carrying his gun, confronted her in the kitchen, and snarled, "Do you have a problem with that?" Denise knew it was time to leave the marriage.

After the second divorce, Denise hit rock bottom. For the next few months, she was a wreck, questioning everything about her life. She was in her early thirties and had not progressed very far in her career or in her personal life. It all seemed to have been a big waste. It was only after months of self-assessment and grieving that Denise was able to start on a growth path. Intuitively, she recognized she needed to make some significant changes in her life by dealing with unresolved issues from her past. Though she probably wouldn't have articulated it this way at the time, Denise was searching for a way to speak unspoken truths, to make overt the sadness and hurt from her past. Like many people who have reached a low point in their lives, Denise sensed that the root of her problems lay inside rather than outside her.

LEGACY

In many respects, Denise's upbringing was "normal." Though she did move around quite a bit, her family life was nothing out of the ordinary. She did not experience any physical abuse, her parents didn't go through an acrimonious divorce, and the household she grew up in ran fairly smoothly. Like most people, however, Denise developed certain skills and carried certain baggage into adulthood because of how she was raised.

Denise had good communication, social, and analytical skills, as well as an ability to get things done despite formidable obstacles; she was also an excellent negotiator. Denise's communication skills resulted from the way she always tried to talk her parents into being happy, her social skills from the constant moving and adapting to new environments, and the analytical skills from trying to figure out why things weren't going right. She learned how to persevere because she felt others in her family were dependent on her to come through for them, and her "fixer" role helped her become a good negotiator.

Her emotional baggage includes being a caretaker in relationships. Denise automatically assumes that when someone is unhappy, she has to try to help them feel better, just as she tried to do with her parents. Part and parcel of this caretaker role is a fear of confrontation. Her mother never confronted her father about any of the major issues in their lives, always attempting to shield him from the children's problems or other household matters. Because no one modeled confronting behavior for her, Denise grew up lacking this skill.

Denise also had low self-esteem, the result of a lack of feedback from her family. The damage people suffer as children isn't always because of what's done to them; it can result from omission of something that should have been there. In Denise's case, the only real feedback she received from her parents was that she wasn't working hard enough to make things right. Other than that, she rarely received compliments or helpful advice. In the absence of constructive feedback, Denise did what all children do: She filled in the "blanks" with her own self-criticism: "I must have done something wrong—or I didn't do enough—or they would have said something to me. . . ."

The strongest drive in Denise's life was to avoid disappointing her parents. As an adult, Denise tried to avoid disappointing everyone—everyone but herself. Put another way, Denise's *familiar* was going all out to please everyone but ending up pleasing no one. She's done this with her husbands and her daughter, and, as we'll see, she's done it in spades at work.

INTERNAL AWARENESS

After her second divorce, Denise was in a great deal of pain, and that pushed her to stop viewing everything in terms of external issues and start exploring internal ones. Up until that point, Denise had compartmentalized her life. She had one personality as a worker, one as a mother, one as a sibling, and one as a daughter. Compartmentalizing kept Denise focused on external things. If there was a problem at work, she could blame the boss. If there was a problem as a mother, she could blame her daughter ("She's driving me nuts, I don't know what's wrong with her"). By setting up external scapegoats as the cause of her problems, Denise avoided facing the internal thread undermining all her relationships. Or she could turn the blame on herself and say, "I just have to work harder to get the boss to approve of me," (or work harder as a mother to get her daughter to behave).

After her second marriage failed, she intuitively began to look inward rather than outward for explanations. It's important to emphasize here that neither I nor anyone in my group had worked with Denise at this point; she was not raised in an environment where psychoanalysis or any type of emotional therapy was viewed positively; she did not receive any sort of professional encouragement to look inward rather than outward. In fact, Denise's friends and family encouraged her to blame her unbalanced second husband for her problems.

Despite all this, Denise instinctively and courageously looked inward. Many people believe that this inward-looking exploration requires some special skill or the guidance of a professional. While the latter may be helpful, it's not always necessary. Denise, like many people, was perfectly capable of facing her internal issues; she just had to reach a point in her life when she was willing to take the risk to do so.

She began asking herself: "What's the repeating pattern or common theme in all these compartmentalized roles that makes me unhappy and not as successful as I'd like to be?" When reflecting on this question, it dawned on Denise that she couldn't control her or other people's disappointment; what she could control was expressing *her* disappointment. Up until this point, she had kept her disappointment to herself. The people in her life had no idea where she was coming from, and by refraining from telling them when she was hurt or disappointed, she ensured that she wouldn't get her needs met. When she tried and failed to please people, she ended up dissatisfied. This was tremendously familiar. Unconsciously, she set up situations as an adult that ensured she wouldn't receive feedback. Her roles as caretaker and fixer guaranteed that she wouldn't have to express her disappointment and receive the feedback that came with this expression.

When Denise began to understand these issues, she was starting to explore the Internal Frontier, and that led to her breakthrough.

PERSONAL–PROFESSIONAL CONNECTION

Denise had been working for her current employer for months before she made a major breakthrough. Up until then, she had started taking small risks, especially in the area of asking for feedback. Denise was one of the first people at the company to take advantage of accountability groups to deal with her difficult client. She recognized that her people constantly whined and complained about the client, and that it did them no good. She used the group to get feedback from the six people who reported to her and said, "I can't help you work effectively with the client unless you tell me how I can work effectively with you. I need to know what I'm doing right and what I'm doing wrong."

On the surface, this may not seem like much of a risk. After all, people say these types of things to their employees every day. But to understand the risk for Denise, you need to know what her *familiar* told her she'd hear after making her seemingly innocuous request: "You're not competent to deal with this client. There's nothing you can do to help the situation because they're just impossible to deal with." This is what she expected to hear because it was the same message she received growing up: *You can't do anything to make us feel better.*

Denise also took the risk of confronting her boss. Again, this might not seem like a big deal to an outsider. It's only when you realize that her boss was a clear symbol for her father that the difficulty of confronting him becomes apparent. His military background, intimidating presence, and the way he ordered rather than requested recalled her father in a number of ways. Denise was aware that her immediate reaction to her boss—her desire to please him rather than express her objections when she knew he was wrong—had everything to do with her past rather than her present. This awareness gave her the courage to sit down with her boss and tell him she disagreed with him without fearing the world would end if she did so. In a number of instances, she voiced her objections to the way he dealt with their problematic client, and when he followed her lead, problems were handled more effectively than they had been in the past.

Still, it wasn't until Denise confronted her mother that she experienced a breakthrough at work and became significantly more effective as a manager. Denise says it was one of the hardest things she had ever done in her life. She talked to her mother about how unhappy she was growing up, how she felt like a victim and a failure at fixing the family, and how her mother had modeled this behavior in the way she interacted with Denise's father. Denise was speaking the unspoken truth when she expressed the big family secret: that Mom was unhappy and a victim. No one dared talk about it at the time, but Denise was finally able to talk about it.

Expressing these feelings—making the covert overt—was liberating. It would have been liberating even if Denise didn't confront her mother directly; she could have written her feelings in an unsent letter or verbalized them to someone else. It is the expression that's important, not to whom it's expressed.

Once Denise experienced these feelings, she broke through to a new level of work productivity and satisfaction. This was most clearly apparent in her approach to the company's most difficult client. When Denise first began working with this client, she did what others had done before her: She tried to please them. This approach just made the client even more abusive and demanding. Once Denise had expressed her feelings to her mother, however, she was willing to confront the client. After all, the sky hadn't fallen when she had talked to her mother. It would be infinitely easier to confront a client than her mother.

Denise also had established growth relationships within her organization that held her accountable and pushed her to take risks. When she talked about the problems she was having with this client, a colleague would challenge her, asking, "Why are you letting this client destroy you and your people?" She'd also done a good job of defining her values. Integrity is one of those values, and it has helped her set limits as to the lines she refuses to cross. One of those lines is taking abuse from this client, and she's firm enough in this value that she decided she'd prefer working somewhere else rather than have to cave in to the client's unreasonable demands.

Internally, Denise had reached a place where she was aware of her tendency to reproduce the *familiar*. This client gave her the perfect opportunity to try to please them and fail, just as she had failed to please her family growing up. To her credit, Denise started to resist this opportunity. She began setting limits with the client. She pushed back at them in a way she had never done with anyone else of significance in her life. If they made ridiculous demands on her or her people or overreacted to a minor problem, she would call them on it.

Her willingness to confront and express her feelings not only has improved the client relationship—they respect Denise's "guts" and ability to cut to the chase—but it has helped Denise and her group work more productively on the client's behalf. Her people spend far less time complaining about the client and more energy on problem-solving.

USING THE PROCESS

While Denise began exploring the Internal Frontier intuitively after her second divorce, her change and growth were greatly facilitated by having a formal process to continue this exploration. Denise's use of accountability groups and relationship-building, for instance, has been critical. Defining her values—especially her recognition of how important integrity is to her—has helped her make key decisions regarding her client. Denise has also employed the grieving process to say good-bye to her old identity, the person who was always miserable and tried to fix everyone around her. It was sad bidding farewell to someone with whom Denise was so familiar, but using a formal method of grieving helped her do so.

Though Denise has come a long way in her growth and development, she's well aware that this is an ongoing process. Change isn't linear. Denise, like everyone else, slips back into the old *familiar*. Certain triggers push her back to that place. There are times when the symbols in her life are evoked by her boss or her client, and she finds herself trying to please and avoid any type of confrontation. To avoid slipping back to that *familiar* too often or for too long a period of time, Denise needs to be acutely alert to her triggers and tendencies. This is where the formal Internal Frontier process helps.

For example, Denise talks about experiencing periods of intense and seemingly inexplicable sadness. Many times, these periods directly follow an achievement of some sort—buying a beautiful home she never thought she could afford, a triumph at work, and so on. If she lets these feelings drag her down—if she unconsciously decides to avoid achievement because it makes her feel so sad—then Denise is going to get stuck. The notion of contrast places, however, helps her understand why she's feeling paradoxically sad. She grasps the fact that it has to do with this question: If she's so valued by her employer now, why couldn't her family have valued her in the same way? Rather than allow these contrast places to have a negative impact on her life, Denise asks the process question: *Is there anything in the present that warrants my feeling this way?*

Still, resisting the *familiar* is a constant battle of alertness. The *familiar* is not like an old car you can trade in for a newer, better model. To a certain extent, you're stuck with it for the rest of your life. The Internal Frontier process is designed to dilute its impact and the frequency with which you fall into it. It also gives you alternative, healthier responses to the old behaviors to which your *familiar* leads you to.

As part of the process, Denise has worked at recognizing these behaviors and correcting them. Based on her internal work, Denise is aware that she has trouble pushing back at intimidating people and that she often falls into caretaking relationships. This awareness doesn't stop Denise from doing these things sometimes. But it does help her catch herself sooner and stop acting in a particularly damaging way. By being alert and relying on the process, Denise will stop reproducing the *familiar* so often, the intensity of its impact will lessen, and she'll be able to extricate herself from it more quickly.

This process has all sorts of payoffs for Denise at work. Recently, Denise was promoted to a new position and had to find someone to take her old job. After interviewing a number of people, she decided on Hal, a very talented person who worked for her and whom she liked a lot. After three months in the new job, however, Hal resigned. It was a difficult three months, because as hard as Denise and Hal tried to make it click, it was clear he was ill-suited for the position. The "old" Denise would have left it there, back at her *familiar* of trying and failing to please someone. This time, however, Denise and Hal sat down and discussed it. It was a difficult, emotional conversation, but it was also illuminating. As it turned out, Hal had little interest in the position but he had felt "compelled" to accept it simply because it was offered; he said his friends had told him it would be "career suicide" to turn the job down, and he tried to rationalize away his doubts by telling himself he would grow into the position. He also told Denise that he had taken the job partly to make her happy. He, like Denise, was a pleaser. Both Hal and Denise were very open and vulnerable in their conversation, Denise admitting her disappointment in how it turned out, but also communicating how much she valued his skills.

As a result of that conversation, Denise found another, more appropriate job for him in the organization, and he's now highly productive and on a growth track. Without understanding the process and using its tools of self-disclosure and openness in relationships,

Denise would have avoided the painful conversation or handled it ineffectively. Because of the self-discovery work she'd done, however, Denise was able to retain and develop a talented and productive employee.

Denise has come a long way in both her personal and professional life. She has much clearer goals than at any other point in her life. They revolve around appreciating and enjoying the fruits of her professional success by creating a personal lifestyle that contains key elements which are important to her. She is also pursuing her vision, which focuses on creating work environments that are meaningful and relationship-driven. Her work on herself has made this much more achievable. She would not have been able to pursue this path without identifying and confronting her old *familiar*, taking the huge risk of trying out new and foreign behaviors, and trusting herself to stay open to the possibility of living and thriving in a new *familiar*.

CHAPTER 12

CHRIS: GREAT GOALS ONLY GET YOU SO FAR

PROFESSIONAL HISTORY

At twenty-nine, Chris has achieved an income level and degree of success that are unusual for someone his age. In 1997, he grossed $220,000 as an insurance agent for a well-known company in a large city, and he expects to gross $350,000 in 1998. He also has accumulated $500,000 in an equity account. Chris has had a full-time assistant for the last four years, and he is planning on hiring at least two other people soon as part of an ambitious expansion strategy. This strategy is driven in part by Chris's desire to purchase an $850,000 home, and he needs to achieve a certain income level to qualify for a loan needed to make the purchase.

Chris has been an insurance agent with this same company for seven years, joining right after he graduated from college. Targeting a highly affluent market, Chris—like many people in the insurance business—started slowly, building contacts, learning the products, and gradually building a base of customers. In the last two years, his practice has taken off, more than doubling his 1995 gross income of $105,000.

Chris has always been an entrepreneurial dynamo. In fact, in college he created a successful mail-order business, and an association named him one of the top 100 college entrepreneurs his senior year. Through this and other ventures as well as scholarships, Chris not only paid for all his college education, but made a profit. In high school, Chris worked as many hours as he could at a local fast-food restaurant to help his struggling family. Hard work, setting and achieving ambitious goals, and a great capacity to plan for the future have characterized Chris's work achievements since adolescence.

PERSONAL HISTORY

Born in a small Midwestern town where most of the people who are raised there remain their entire lives, Chris recalls it being an idyllic place until he was ten. Up until that time, he and his sister lived in a nice farmhouse, their dad ran a farm-supply equipment store, and their mother was a homemaker. It was a safe, pretty, homogeneous place, and Chris has fond memories of his childhood.

Then their house burned down. They were visiting relatives when they received the call, returning in time to find the volunteer fire department futilely fighting the flames. They all stood there watching the house burn to the ground with everything they owned inside. Though Chris didn't know this at the time, his father had no insurance, and his mother never forgave him for this irresponsible act. After the fire, she, Chris, and Chris's sister all had to work at the local fast-food restaurant to help make ends meet. Again, Chris didn't know this back then, but shortly after the fire, his mother began an affair with a neighbor whose child she sometimes baby-sat.

Chris felt humiliated by the circumstances to which they were reduced. He remembers wearing secondhand clothes from the Salvation Army and generally being deprived of things other kids took for granted. Though Chris was a good kid who worked hard at school and at his after-school job, he often fought with his sister, who was as rebellious as Chris was status quo–conscious. He clearly recalls that he was viewed as the "good kid" and she was seen as the "bad one."

His dad, who had never been particularly dependable, was even less so after the fire. His farming-supply store grew shabbier and produced less income. Chris felt as if his father was completely out of it, uninvolved in family issues. When his mother would berate him for his indolence and apathy, he would just leave the room. While his father would often talk enthusiastically about his dreams for the future, he never did anything about them. Chris recalls being ashamed of and disappointed in his father. He seemed oblivious to everything.

When Chris was older, his mom and dad divorced. While his mom remarried and adopted her new husband's daughter, his dad regressed even more and spent most of his time traveling in a pickup truck between his home and his own mother's home. After Chris had graduated from college and was living in a nice section of the city where he worked, his father paid him an unannounced visit. Chris wasn't home when he arrived, so his father spent the night sleeping in his truck, much to the consternation of Chris's upper-middle-class neighbors.

Having worked hard all his life, Chris has begun enjoying the fruits of his labors in recent years—buying an expensive car, a nice townhouse, and other status symbols. While he has achieved certain financial goals, Chris remains single. He's been frustrated with his inability to enter into a committed relationship with a woman, and he only has a few strong—and relatively recent—friendships with men.

LEGACY

As you might imagine, one of the main skills Chris derived from his upbringing was an ability to look beyond present problems and envision a better future. The childhood fire that wiped out his family, the feuds with his sister, the unresponsiveness of his father—all made for a number of grim years. He learned how to persevere, and this helped him a great deal when he started in the insurance business. Those first few years weed a lot of young people out of the business; they become fed up with the grind of making thousands of calls and not getting anyone to talk to them. Chris made it through these early years because he was driven by his vision of the future. He stuck with it because he was convinced things would get better.

Chris also has tremendous initiative and is great at taking charge of a situation rather than depending on others. Growing up, Chris was the most responsible person in the family. His father was ineffectual, his mother was caught up in blaming and feeling sorry for herself, and his sister was rebellious. Chris was the responsible one; he was the person who brought home good grades and good money. Planning and goal-setting were integral to Chris's role. He learned that if he planned carefully, he could achieve future goals—his planning helped achieve his goal of financing his college education.

One aspect of Chris's legacy is his "go-getter" attitude. He looks and acts like the classic American success story come to life, a good-looking, clean-cut guy who is determined to be successful at any cost. He fits the

Horatio Alger mold, and his planning, goal-setting, hard work, and perseverance are traits handed down from his early years that have stood him in good stead.

At the same time, there's some baggage Chris carries as a result of those years. The most significant issue is his inability to challenge or confront others. When Chris started selling insurance, his managers thought he was a nice guy, but no one would have bet he would succeed to the extent that he has. When Chris started making calls, none of his potential customers took him seriously. He was incapable of asking them for anything; it was difficult for him to ask them for an appointment, let alone challenge or confront them with a request for their business. Chris had succeeded in the past by working hard, and he was working harder than most young agents during the first year or two of his job. He discovered that hard work would only get him so far. The people he was trying to sell to—highly successful, sophisticated professionals—required more than diligence. Chris came off as a nice but superficial guy. He was pleasant to talk to but lacked the relationship skills required to get them to trust him with an insurance program.

Chris's *familiar* is not getting his basic emotional needs met, particularly his need for intimacy. In Chris's family, one of the secrets was that the adults acted like children and one of the children was the functional adult. While this role reversal provided Chris with certain skills, it also caused him to reproduce that familiar feeling of not having people meet his needs. One of the easiest ways to reproduce this feeling is by not telling people what you need, avoiding challenging or confronting them with what you expect from them.

Early in Chris's life, he learned that you don't receive anything unless you do it for yourself. Today, that message translates into: What's the point in asking anyone for anything? Obviously, this self-dependency has made it difficult for him to establish growth-oriented relationships, especially with women. When you have problems expressing feelings like disappointment and anger or expectations of others, you struggle to achieve intimacy and trust in a relationship.

Another piece of baggage from Chris's past is his intolerance and insensitivity to people he perceives as "lazy" or "complainers." Chris has difficulty with people who don't bring the same "success at any cost" mind-set to their work. This makes him a difficult person to work for and can be a major stumbling block in his plans to expand his practice. Chris lacks the ability to empathize with other agents who are struggling to make sales or can't get someone to return their calls. To Chris, the solution is to work longer and harder.

INTERNAL AWARENESS

External goals can drive internal work, and this is what happened in Chris's case. More than anything else, he wanted to do better than his parents; he never again wanted to be as poor and humiliated as he was while growing up. When he started working for the insurance agency, he recognized that he wasn't making progress, and he was eager for his boss and me (I was consulting with the insurance company) to work with him.

Perhaps a bit too eager. In his zeal to deal with personal issues that would help him succeed professionally, Chris initially went a little off course as he worked on the Internal Frontier. For instance, we had talked to him about looking for behavioral patterns that might help him identify his *familiar*. As a result, he created a flowchart of all the women he had dated. On the chart he listed the name of the woman, the amount of time they had gone out, the cause of the breakup, who initiated it, and the values they had in common. When he showed us the chart, he acknowledged that he knew the chart was "kind of strange" but that he was using it to look for patterns that might explain why he was having trouble establishing long-term, committed relationships. While Chris's impulse to keep the chart was healthy, the impulse was also indicative of his problem: He reduced intimate relationships to an analysis of a flowchart.

Still, Chris was willing to explore his internal issues, and he established relationships with both me and his boss and began to see how his upbringing had impacted who he was today. But perhaps the most important first step he took was convening his own personal board of directors. This had been a half-serious suggestion from his boss that Chris embraced wholeheartedly. The idea was that Chris would ask two or three of his clients and some other businesspeople he had met to serve on his board in exchange for a free dinner. All he would ask from them would be feedback. For Chris, this was asking a lot. All his life, he had refrained from asking others for anything, preferring to do it all himself. Now he was willing to take the moderate risk of asking people he respected and valued for help.

This was just the right level of risk for Chris. He wasn't ready to sit down with another businessperson in a one-on-one relationship and ask, "What am I doing wrong?" It would have been even riskier for him to approach a personal friend and ask how he came across. Chris wasn't able to take that big of a step at that point. People need to take manageable risks, and creating a personal board of directors was one Chris could handle. The worst that might happen was that someone would decline to be on his board, and Chris could explain that rejection in business terms and wouldn't take it personally.

By creating this board, Chris discovered that contrary to his *familiar*, other people could meet his needs. Though it was unsettling to put himself in the position of developing trusting relationships with others, it resulted in a significant amount of new business for Chris. Part of this was simply because the people on Chris's board proved to be a great source of referrals. But Chris also was becoming more aware of his difficulty in forming relationships and asking for help, and that awareness made him more willing to confront and challenge his prospects.

THE PERSONAL–PROFESSIONAL CONNECTION

The linkages between Chris's personal and professional life loop back and forth in particularly interesting ways. At the beginning of his career, his personal issues made it difficult for him to make much professional headway; his *familiar* feeling of not getting his needs met caused Chris to place strict limits on what he'd ask from others. Once he achieved a certain amount of professional success, however, he became dissatisfied with his personal life— his inability to sustain a long-term, meaningful relationship. Like many young, successful people, he looked at all the professional progress he'd made and asked: Why can't I have the same success in my personal life?

It's a good question, because if Chris can achieve that personal success, it will kick back and give him the impetus to achieve even more ambitious professional goals. For Chris to make it to the next level of success and effectiveness, he needs to experience deep feelings and be intimately connected to another person. This has been difficult for Chris to do. It's not that he has no friends or people dislike him. In fact, Chris is very likable, but he's the type of person who is everyone's buddy but no one's close friend.

Chris's progress in his career is directly proportional to his level of vulnerability and openness with other people. As he's learned to form growth relationships with male colleagues and clients, he's made a quantum leap in selling effectiveness. To understand this connection, you should understand that Chris is involved in relationship sales; he is not a transactional salesperson trying to close a deal by offering the lowest price. He's interacting with clients who are looking for millions of dollars in insurance. If they don't trust him, they won't buy from him. In this arena, insurance agents aren't yes-men (or women) for their clients; they express their feelings to them, they demand things of them, and they establish reciprocal relationships. In other words, they create a high level of intimacy.

Chris has done this to a certain extent, but he still has a way to go. We're working with him on creating the same type of openness and vulnerability in his relationships with women that he has with men. One of the assignments we recently gave him indicates how he's going about this task. For a number of months, Chris has been dating a woman he really likes. Though they have a great time together, she sometimes throws up barriers that prevent the relationship from evolving. In the past, Chris would never challenge someone about this type of behavior. Chris's assignment is to confront her about the relationship, and say something to the effect of "I'd like you to open up and trust me enough so that we can develop a truly intimate relationship rather than one that avoids real intimacy. If you want that as much as I do, then we both have to start taking some risks and open up to each other. If you don't want that kind of relationship, let's end it now."

Chris is asking her to make the relationship emotionally reciprocal (rather than activity reciprocal). It's much easier for Chris—and much more familiar—to attempt to please the women he's going out with and try to make sure everything is going smoothly. What's problematic for him is to demand that he get something back on an emotional level.

If he can do this (not just in this instance, but continuously), Chris can move up to a new level of success. To sell bigger policies, he needs to establish relationships with an even more affluent client base. These people demand even more trust, reciprocity, and open communication than his current clients. If he can establish an emotionally reciprocal relationship with a woman he dates, it will dilute the power of his old *familiar*. The gender difference and the fact that it's a personal relationship doesn't matter. The *familiar* cuts across these distinctions. Personal relationships are where Chris is stuck, and if he can break through in this part of his life, it will translate into professional growth.

As Chris learns to establish greater trust and intimacy in his relationships, it will also make him a better manager of people. Chris has highly ambitious goals—he wants to gross $750,000 by the year 2000—and he can't achieve them if he tries to do everything himself. It's not just a matter of turning over clerical details to an assistant. Chris needs to trust others sufficiently so that he can give them meaty assignments and not second-guess and micromanage them every step of the way. Certainly he's going to have to take risks in the professional area of his life, but it's going to be difficult for him to do so unless he takes risks in his important personal relationships.

USING THE PROCESS

Contrast places can be a serious blocker for Chris if he's not alert. When he was growing up, his parents held no great expectations for him. In fact, he rarely received any encouragement or approval for his diligence and hard work. When his mom recently visited him, she saw the luxury car in front of Chris's home but refused to believe that it was actually Chris's car; she couldn't imagine her son being so successful that he could afford this type of automobile.

Sometimes Chris has trouble imagining the same thing. As one of the top ten performers in his organization, he received an all-expenses-paid trip to Hawaii. As part of the package, Chris stayed at an exclusive resort, and when he was there he found himself wondering if he were dreaming. He was in a place that was far removed from both his hometown and his parents' expectations for him.

There are times when Chris will leave a meeting—a meeting at which he has given a client useful advice or sold a policy—and he'll "feel like a fraud." He's convinced he's not as good as his clients think he is; he's certain that his advice is mediocre or that the policy he sold wasn't the right one. "Who am I to be giving these highly successful people advice?" he asks himself. Chris settles into a dark, despairing funk at these times, and he needs to realize that he's in a contrast place. Awareness of what's happening—that there's nothing in the present to justify his feelings—is crucial. If he takes these feelings as permanent, he'll avoid selling even bigger policies or advising clients on more important matters, because these actions will make him feel like an even bigger fraud. As long as Chris keeps reminding himself that his feelings are rooted in the past rather than the present, he'll be able to stop them from blocking him.

Chris has also grieved the loss of who he was, not only in relation to his family but also to friends he met when he first started his job. He's grown at a phenomenal rate and left a number of people behind, and he's expressed his sadness about this fact to me and the head of his agency's office. When Chris was a boy, one of the secrets in his family was that he was the unacknowledged adviser. Now Chris's relationship with his family is that he's the acknowledged adviser—they come to him with questions about investments and other matters. Chris is doing a great job of making the covert overt; he talks about how he always acted like an adult and rarely got to feel like a child. Speaking the unspoken truth gives Chris a way to grieve the sadness of this early role. Similarly, when Chris first moved to the city where he works, he made a number of friends who haven't grown much over the years. Leaving them behind hasn't been easy because they were important to him when he first arrived in town, but it's clear his relationships with them are doomed because of their unequal rates of growth. Rather than allowing them to keep him stuck, he used the grieving process to move on.

The *familiar* is crucial for Chris to keep in mind, not only so he can progress in his career, but so he can enjoy his success. Chris will continue to reproduce the familiar feeling of unmet needs if he only focuses on achieving his external goals. As Chris says, "I get so caught up in doing that I stop being." What's comfortable and familiar for Chris is intense, nonstop activity. It doesn't leave time for relationships, and Chris can end up as lonely now as he was growing up. Chris is trying to enjoy who he is and what he has. To enjoy this "being" part of himself, Chris needs to develop and maintain reciprocal relationships. These relationships are places where he can simply be who he is by expressing his deep feelings and receiving feedback about them.

Chris has come so far so fast in part because of his natural ability to envision the future and create goals that keep him moving toward that vision. But his vision and goals aren't enough. The challenge for Chris is how close he is willing to get to people within a relationship. Is he willing to cause others discomfort? Is he able to confront them? Can he allow himself to disappoint them? If Chris is going to continue growing, these are the issues he has to work on. Disappointing others is an especially high hurdle, since Chris was the designated non-disappointer in his family. Surrounded by people who frequently disappointed the other family members, Chris didn't feel he had the option of letting anyone else down. Certainly that's helped him achieve what he's achieved to date; he works like a demon to meet other people's needs. But it's also what will hold him back. Once he takes the scary step of disappointing someone he cares about, then Chris will realize the world doesn't screech to a halt when this happens. When Chris recognizes that disappointment is an integral, acceptable part of any healthy relationship, he'll be more willing to open himself up to intimacy in both his personal and professional lives.

CHAPTER 13

BILL: CONFRONTING THE ONES YOU CARE ABOUT MOST

PROFESSIONAL HISTORY

Bill heads a large office of a premier investment brokerage house. A senior partner since 1989, he has built a highly successful operation with about 115 brokers and a support and clerical staff of about 100. Not surprisingly, Bill at age forty-five already has had considerable financial success; his 1997 income was about $1.5 million. Along the way, Bill has achieved legendary status within the industry. His legend is not only a result of his rapid rise to the top of a tough business, but because of his prowess as a motivator, evidenced by his ability to create an environment in which the brokers who work for him produce at levels higher than they themselves ever had anticipated.

Bill's entire professional life has been dedicated to the brokerage business. After graduating from college, he immediately went to work as a stockbroker at a branch office of the firm for which he has worked ever since. His outstanding production, coupled with the leadership qualities he exhibited early on, put him on a fast track. After three years, he transferred to another of the firm's branch offices, where he was in charge of recruiting and training brokers. Then he was moved to second in command at one of the largest offices of the same firm, where he essentially served as chief operating officer in charge of day-to-day operations. He stayed in that position for five years, earning up to $400,000 a year while still in his early thirties. But he never was promoted to the position of senior partner in charge of that office. To reach that level, he had to move to his current position: running a major-market office that was struggling until he came along. Seven years later, it's the firm's flagship operation, serving the investment needs of some of the nation's wealthiest individuals.

PERSONAL HISTORY

Bill was born and raised in a series of communities on the Eastern seaboard, where his father also was an executive in the brokerage business. Like Bill, his father landed on a management track right away and worked in the company's home office for thirteen years. In addition to being highly driven and a very hard worker, Bill's father was a functional alcoholic. In a pattern not unusual for his generation, Bill's father drank a great deal but always showed up for work. He did what was necessary to take care of business and advance his career, but drinking heavily was part of his daily routine.

When Bill was a child, he needed brain surgery for a tumor. At the time, he was not expected to live through the surgery because of the location of the tumor. "If he survives without paralysis, it will be a miracle," his family was told. The procedure took nineteen hours, but survive he did, and the only souvenir was a scar on his forehead. The cruel mocking by neighborhood kids was a constant reminder of his plight.

"The people making fun of you have the problem," his father would reassure him, "not you." As helpful as his father's emotional support was back then, it didn't last due to his father's drinking. As Bill was entering adolescence, his father began to turn on the family. He never had been easy to deal with, but he began to belittle his wife, Bill's brother and sister, and Bill himself. No one ever has determined what the catalyst was—Bill thinks it may have been a career disappointment—but from that point on his relationship with his family was characterized by bitterness and a series of personal attacks. His father's anger could surface at any time and be directed at any convenient target.

Though Bill believes his mother didn't have as much influence on his life as his father did, he recognizes how important her role was in the family dynamic. Bill describes his mother as a traditional housewife: loving, nurturing, and a very caring parent. Like many women of her generation, she didn't challenge her husband's drinking. Instead, she adapted to it, living in denial with her husband, who to this day still refuses to admit he's an alcoholic. Rather than confront her husband when he would launch into one of his booze-soaked tirades, she would respond by withdrawing. So Bill began to take up for her. When he was an adolescent, Bill tried to defend her from his tirades. "That's enough," he would say to his father. "Leave her alone." But it didn't have much impact.

A telling incident occurred much earlier, when Bill was only three or four years old, but he still remembers it vividly. He was sitting on the second-floor landing in his pajamas, listening to his parents argue in the kitchen. Though Bill was too young to intervene directly, he suddenly was struck by the need to do something, so he did the only thing that came to mind: He flung himself from the landing down the flight of stairs, rolling into the living room not far from where his parents were arguing. They were so consumed by their fight that they didn't even notice him tumbling down the stairs. They never left the kitchen, nor did they pay any attention at all to him. Bill felt like he didn't exist. He simply picked himself up, dusted himself off, climbed back up the stairs and went to sleep.

As you can imagine, the impact of this incident on Bill was greater than the stairs on his body. Hurt and frustrated by his father's treatment of him over the years, Bill resolved early on that nothing his father said would get to him. In fact, nothing infuriated Bill's father more than his inability to get a rise out of Bill no matter what he said or did.

Bill is a very different type of father and husband than his father was. After graduating from an excellent college and entering the workforce, Bill married his college sweetheart. They now have four children, and he's developed strong emotional bonds with each of them. His relationship with his wife is also solid, and while they've had some rocky times, they've both grown together. Though they've argued like any married couple, the arguments were not the one-sided, hostile fights that his mother and father engaged in.

Bill has changed his habits over the years. Early in his adult life, he had problems with both alcohol and money, drinking and spending too much. Despite his rapidly rising income, Bill managed to spend more than he made (on homes, cars, trips, and other luxuries), resulting in problems in paying his taxes on time. In recent years, he's stopped drinking and controlled his spending, though he still lives a relatively lavish lifestyle. He also spends much more time with his family, setting aside Saturdays as his kids' day and not allowing work to interfere with the new tradition that he has established.

LEGACY

As the oldest sibling in an alcohol-dominated home, Bill has grown up to be someone who is brilliant at helping others fulfill their potential. This may seem like an odd legacy, considering that Bill failed to stop his father from flying off the handle and taking it out on him and his mother. Though his childhood efforts were futile—his tumble down the stairs was highly symbolic of that futility—they evolved into an impulse to help those who were struggling. Even more significantly, interacting with an abusive alcoholic provided Bill with the ingenuity and quick-thinking skills necessary to deal effectively with other people. When you live with someone capable of spinning into a towering rage without any apparent provocation, you learn to think on your feet. You develop skills that help you survive these outbursts. Bill became adept at keeping his father from doing greater harm than he did, "coaching" his mother and siblings so that they didn't trigger a fit of temper.

Bill is an incredibly quick study who is able to read a situation and cut to the chase faster than anyone I ever have worked with, a common legacy for children from alcoholic and abusive homes. These people learn at a tender age how to deal with highly volatile situations, and they use their wits to survive. Bill doesn't get thrown by complex business situations or pressures to meet ambitious goals. Just as he learned to assess the environment in his home instantly and make quick decisions that enabled him to survive his father's wrath, he can size up a business situation in a flash and make astute decisions.

The baggage that comes with this upbringing is manifested most clearly in Bill's personal and professional relationships. Bill has always had a difficult time expressing love and sharing feelings in intimate relationships. He has been a good husband and father, but dealing with the intimate aspects of these relationships has been a challenge. As a child, no one modeled for Bill the openness, trust, and vulnerability that are the hallmarks of intimate relationships. In the early years of his marriage, Bill found it difficult to express his feelings directly and continuously to his wife and children. In a very real sense, Bill substituted material possessions for emotionally valuable relationships.

Bill has also carried this baggage into his professional life. For many years, he had difficulty establishing reciprocal relationships. Though he's always been superb at motivating others, he hasn't always been skilled in distinguishing growth-oriented relationships from dependent ones. Before Bill transferred to his current position, he was second in command at a major office of the brokerage for four years. The senior partner had led Bill to believe he would have the opportunity to take over the top position, but it became clear that the other man had no intention of folding his tent in favor of Bill. Even so, Bill deluded himself into believing that the man would do what he had agreed to, although it was becoming increasingly obvious that the promotion would never happen.

Just as Bill didn't confront his father about his alcoholism and temper when he was growing up, he was unable to confront his boss for years about his inference that Bill would attain the top spot. Bill's *familiar* was not wanting to see how fruitless it was to hope that his father could meet his needs and validate him. It was too painful to see how lopsided and unrewarding the relationship was. Consequently, he couldn't see that the relationship with the senior partner was a one-way street; he couldn't demand accountability from the office head, just as he couldn't demand accountability from his father.

INTERNAL AWARENESS

Though Bill had done some self-discovery work when he was younger, his real breakthrough came when he was thirty-four. It was the result of a confrontation Bill had with his father, and a series of discussions Bill and I were having about his future. We talked about the position he was stuck in as second in command of the brokerage office, and I observed that he could be there a long time. His boss clearly was not going to make room for Bill to get the promotion he richly deserved. Bill talked about his fervent belief that he had to run his own shop to fulfill his vision as an exceptional developer of people. He articulated this belief to me after his boss had intimated that he might become senior partner in one of several extremely unappealing markets that lacked customer bases worth developing. Bill had no desire to head any of those offices, knowing he needed a market with greater potential.

It was important for Bill to understand how his relationship with Mark, his boss, was tied to failing to get his emotional needs met as a child. What Bill came to realize was that just as he was ignored by his father, he received little credit for his office's accomplishments—the lion's share of acclaim went to Mark. Significantly, Mark also gave Bill the task of firing unsuccessful brokers, a task that Mark (and Bill) loathed. Every time a broker had to be fired, Bill's boss suddenly left town, forcing Bill to clean up the mess. Bill felt unappreciated, so he often gave himself material rewards—a trip, a car—instead of demanding the recognition he deserved. Whenever he turned to his boss for feedback, all he would receive was a vague, circuitous response that failed to acknowledge his contributions. His boss never said, "Bill, you're doing a tremendous job. Your contribution is enormous, and the main reason our business has skyrocketed is because you have made our brokers the best in the business." The only way he could reward Bill was by paying him a lot of money, but as with his father, the emotional support was missing. Neither validated who Bill was. His father and his boss were very talented executives—Bill credits the vision his boss brought to his work for much of the office's success—but neither had any interest in developing people. It eventually dawned on Bill that his relationship with his boss exactly modeled the relationship with his father, and this was part of his growing internal awareness.

After years of avoiding the issue that lay between them, it was time for Bill to confront his boss. Such a confrontation, however, was a huge risk for Bill, and not only because his superior was a highly respected presence who had built a strong office. The senior partner was a clear symbol for Bill's father, and after a number of discussions, Bill became aware of a crucial bit of information: To confront his boss, he would first have to confront his father. In reality, Bill could have found other ways of expressing his feelings that would have been just as effective as a direct confrontation; given Bill's personality, however, this direct approach was the appropriate action for him.

Bill decided to orchestrate an intervention with the entire family present, and he brought together the family—parents, brother, and sister—without telling anyone what it was about. It took every ounce of energy and perseverance Bill could muster, and he felt himself losing resolve and backing out any number of times the night before. Still, he went through with it. The main point of the intervention was to confront his father about his alcoholism, but during the meeting no one besides Bill was able to deal with the seriousness of the situation. True to form, his father denied everything, particularly the drinking that made his life so difficult and threatened the family for so many years. He acted as though he had no idea what Bill was talking about. Bill's mother was uncomfortable and embarrassed about the situation.

The entire family was unwilling to speak the unspoken. The family secret could not be acknowledged. The power of the *familiar* was so strong that they preferred the old comfortable feeling of helplessness over dealing with the truth.

For Bill, though, the experience was revelatory. By expressing his deepest feelings to his father—by talking about the sadness and hurt he felt as a child—he was able to move on. Articulating all this removed the obstacle that kept him terrified of confronting others with his feelings. Bill learned that the sky didn't fall when he told his father how he felt. If the world didn't end at that point, it certainly wouldn't end when he talked to the head of his office.

The discussion was difficult. Bill's boss viewed Bill's desire to leave the office as a personal betrayal; he thought Bill was ungrateful for refusing to accept a position as head of a smaller office. At the same time, Bill felt indebted to his boss; he'd done a number of things that had helped Bill's career, especially when he was just getting started. When he appealed to Bill's sense of loyalty, it was a powerful appeal. If Bill had not confronted his father, it's likely that the appeal would have worked.

But Bill was adamant. His boss asked me to intervene and convince Bill to stay, explaining to me that he depended on Bill's expertise and support. I told him the split seemed inevitable and that it probably would be the best thing for both of them. Eventually, he came to terms with Bill's need to pursue other opportunities. One of those opportunities involved a No. 1 position: heading the firm's office in one of the nation's wealthiest and most promising markets.

To accept this position meant moving his family across the country to a place where he knew few people. It meant taking over an office with much promise but also many problems. It also meant taking the risk of leaving a relationship with his boss that was intensely familiar. Bill's growing internal awareness allowed him to accept the position and take the risk it entailed.

THE PERSONAL–PROFESSIONAL CONNECTION

Despite its potential, the office Bill took over had been floundering. The previous office head was very bright and committed but incapable of making the tough decisions required to turn things around. When Bill joined in 1989, the challenge was huge. He faced the task of clearing out the deadwood, which meant more dreaded confrontations. More accurately, Bill *used* to dread confrontation. While they still caused him anxiety, he had two major ones under his belt and was willing to take on others.

Within a year of Bill's taking over the office, twenty-six of the office's eighty brokers left, some voluntarily and others involuntarily. Bill trimmed nearly a third of the broker base without any loss of productivity or effectiveness. Using his superior developmental skills, he helped those who remained experience tremendous growth. With his eye for talent, he brought in a number of people who have also made great contributions. Bill not only turned the office around, but he made it one of the highest-performing offices in the company's history. Additionally, he achieved this performance turnaround in record time. When people talk about Bill in his industry, they refer to him as a legend. He regularly lectures around the country, inspiring people with his eloquence and mixture of personal and professional anecdotes.

Bill is articulate in describing the personal–professional connection in his life: "Before I knew myself, I brought needless complexity to everything. My issues and goals were so convoluted that even I couldn't understand them. With self-knowledge, I have a handle on my goals and what I need to do to realize them."

What he needs to do is form reciprocal, accountable relationships and to demand that others do the same. Traditionally, new brokers are bogged down with hundreds of pages of material about the company and its products and policies when they join. As a result, brokers immediately become anxious and confused at a time when they should be focusing on only one thing: building relationships with prospects and clients. Bill has broken with industry tradition and subordinated content training to relationship training.

Similarly, when he has meetings with his brokers, they don't get much face-to-face time. He is incredibly astute at focusing on and communicating a broker's opportunities and challenges quickly, and the brokers typically are stunned by both the alacrity and accuracy of his comments. The boy who had to react immediately to his father's constantly changing moods and sobriety level is today the man who motivates people by rapidly expressing his feelings about their performance, stating his expectations, and helping them identify their blockers. Bill is also highly intolerant of people who give excuses or whine about obstacles. He is a zealot about accountability, and confronts those associates who look outside themselves to divert the blame for poor performance. Those who can't meet his demands leave. But brokers who respond to his counsel and improve their performance usually find they become better at their jobs than they ever thought they could be.

. Bill has always been skilled at developing others. Now, however, he's also good at confronting people about unmet expectations and doing what they promised they'd do. This combination of skills has made it possible for him to achieve incredible success. If he had not done his personal work, he would never have reached this breakthrough level.

USING THE PROCESS

One of Bill's favorite sayings is "Each generation refines the prior generation's neuroses," and he acknowledges that he continues to struggle with issues that are a refinement of his father's. A voracious reader, Bill tends to use his reading as a barrier that separates him from his family. He's prone to hiding behind a book, his favorite way to build emotional distance. But his struggle for self-knowledge has paid off in his strengthened relationship with his family.

Building growth relationships in his personal and professional lives is a critical part of the process for Bill. He needs to be aware of his familiar tendency to avoid the intimacy and confrontation that are part of any growth relationship. By making a conscious effort to form and maintain these relationships, Bill dilutes the power of his *familiar*.

He also needs to be aware of people who serve as symbols in his life. Any powerful figure—a boss, an important customer—can easily return Bill to his *familiar*. Without thinking, he can revert to his nonconfrontational role of failing to get his needs met. Being alert to this possibility is important for Bill.

Maintaining reciprocity in his relationships is another process step that he needs to keep in mind. Bill is great at meeting other people's needs and developing them like crazy, but getting his own needs met is something he can easily neglect. He recalled how for years he had attended a regular reunion with high school friends, and how it was a great deal of fun at first. Over the years, however, he noticed that he was providing his friends a great deal of feedback and receiving none in return. He would challenge one person to deal with a problem in his business and ask questions that would prompt him to find a solution. No one, however, seemed interested in providing him with similar feedback. It occurred to Bill that he had outgrown these people; that he was no longer interested in one-sided relationships.

In both the personal and business arenas, Bill has had to break off relationships that don't give him anything in return. This is difficult; it's hard to acknowledge that old friends have not grown and can no longer meet your needs. Grieving the loss of who he was has helped Bill make this break. He has allowed himself to feel sad over this loss and express his feelings about it within the growth relationships he now has in his life.

Finally, Bill relies on his vision—and the mission, goals, and values attached to it—to guide his actions. That vision—to be a great developer of people—enables him to deliver feedback that has tremendous impact. He knows that to develop people, he can't beat around the bush or avoid dealing with painful issues. He recognizes this truism: Healthy communication is simple, direct, and clear, while neurotic communication is needlessly vague and complex. In the past, Bill might have attempted to cushion his remarks with unclear, generalized comments like "You have to change your attitude about our staff meetings." In contrast, Bill now allows himself to say, "You have to talk less at the staff meetings. Nobody else gets a chance to say anything." Some of the brokers in Bill's charge have attended the finest schools in the country, and a number of them have told me, "I spent years educating myself and complicating things. I've learned more in a year from Bill's ability to reduce things to their essence. Bill's genius is in how he simplifies things."

CHAPTER 14

THE *FAMILIAR* PAST, PRESENT, AND FUTURE

Most books end with a concluding chapter that is nothing more than a summary of the points made in the previous pages. I've always found this practice tiresome and even insulting. Summaries and outlines can be helpful, and I've found they're most useful when I review materials and put them in my own words. This not only personalizes it for me, but it ensures that I truly understand and have integrated what I read. If you feel you need a summary, you'll construct a much more useful one by going through the chapters and creating your own personalized outline.

This last chapter provides you with a broader perspective on the Internal Frontier process, and suggests why this process will become increasingly important in our changing world. In terms of the former, I will track the dynamics of the process through four generations of my own family, and help you track your own family through the generations. It's important to understand that the issues you're dealing with have a broader context than your own life, that they've been handed down and filtered by previous generations, and that you'll hand down and filter messages to the next generation. Seeing

the themes that run through generations is not only fasci-
nating, but it provides you with another tool to understand the personal–professional linkages in your life. I
know it's helped me grieve my losses, celebrate my victo-
ries, and translate personal self-discovery into professional growth and success.

Given this generational theme, it seems fitting to
end the book by examining the trends that will impact all
of us, now and in the future. Let's start, however, by looking at events that took place about a hundred years ago.

A SENSE OF STRUGGLE

Until early adolescence, my grandparents lived in Russia
at a time when anti-Semitism was rampant and pogroms
were common. (A pogrom was an organized assault on
Jewish villages, during which homes were burnt to the
ground and most of the inhabitants were massacred.) At
any moment, their possessions or even their lives could
be taken away. Each day was a struggle for survival, and
it was a struggle to which their parents had adapted. To
my great-grandparents and others in the community, it
was "normal" to be constantly afraid and never believe
the future would be any better.

This sense of struggle was a very literal *familiar* for
all four of my grandparents, and over the course of four
years in the early 1900s they individually made an excru-
ciating decision to break away from it. Between the ages
of twelve and fifteen, they each left home. Taking only
what they could carry and making their way hundreds of
miles to a German port city, they spent the next few
weeks in a freighter's steerage and arrived in a strange
country where they didn't speak the language or know
the customs. They made the decision to leave the people

they most cared about for an unknown and uncomfortable new world. They could have easily decided otherwise; they could have chosen to try to adapt and get along with the lunatics who ruled their country. They were motivated by an innate human impulse for growth and change. Their desire for something better drove them to a country that seemed to offer it. Though they ended up working in sweatshops six days a week rather than striking it rich, their impulse was for a better life, if not for themselves, then for their children.

The struggle and adversity that marked my grandparents' lives also was evident in my parents' lives, though in a mutated form. My father certainly struggled in dental school; as the only Jew in the school, he faced a significant amount of harassment. But his life wasn't threatened and his property wasn't in danger of being confiscated. Still, his *familiar* was struggle, and he worked harder than he ever needed to in order to create it. It was no coincidence that he chose a profession—as a dentist and oral surgeon—where he'd always be on call. Patients would phone in great pain in the middle of the night. My father worked arduous twelve-hour days at a profession that is physically as well as emotionally taxing. While my grandparents worked so hard because they needed to—they sent whatever surplus cash they had to help relatives escape the old country—my father did so because his *familiar* was to struggle. We could have lived nicely on much less money than he made. But for him, the legacy of his parents' struggle was never far from his mind. Consciously, he justified his hard work by saying that he wanted the best for us, and that he had made a commitment to his patients. There was nothing more important in his life than keeping the commitments he made.

He was raised in a way that made it second nature for him to work as if his life depended on it. This was part of the legacy my grandparents gave him. At the same time, my father took risks and broke with his *familiar* in certain ways. The biggest break involved his visits to the racetrack. He was probably the only person I know who bet regularly at the racetrack and came out ahead; he had great willpower and set firm limits for himself, preventing himself from losing too much. My father went to the racetrack because he enjoyed the experience, and this was the risk he took: to have a good time. His decision to marry my mother, who was a dancer, was also a clear break from his *familiar*, and an additional risk to enjoy his life. Her immersion in and commitment to the performing arts was quite different from anything he had previously known, and exposed him to a side of life that balanced his scientific and clinical perspective. My grandfather viewed his son's choice of a mate and his racetrack hobby as indulgences; he was Orthodox in his beliefs and never allowed himself a hobby and rarely a relaxing moment.

Enjoying himself was a big risk for my father, and it's one that paid off in a very important way. In his profession, it helped him build strong and enduring relationships with his patients. Their loyalty to him in many cases spanned almost four decades. I'm also convinced it extended his life. Most of his partners in the practice and many of his colleagues literally worked themselves to death; some of them died in their fifties, and another group not long after that. My father lived to age seventy-seven, and I believe it was due in large part to the risk he took in enjoying himself and bringing some integration to his life. Unlike many of his colleagues, he chose to break with his past to a certain extent and recognize that there was more to life than an obsessive struggle.

The irony in all of this is that my grandparents—by coming to this country and exposing their children to a new culture and better opportunities—gave them the information and experiences they needed to take risks and break with the past. My mother's work as a dancer—she began in ballet, worked in stage shows, and danced in three movies—was nothing short of heresy from my father's parents' perspective, as well as the extended family's.

Similarly, my parents exposed me and my siblings to more educational opportunities and travel, and this exposure provided us with the knowledge we needed to make even more significant breaks with the past. All of us, for instance, married non-Jews, an inconceivable act for previous generations. At the same time, I still struggle in ways that are remarkably similar to my father and grandparents. It's very familiar for me not to enjoy what comes to me relatively easily; I still find it difficult to relax, to set limits on the projects I take on and the hours I work, and to enjoy the fruits of my labor.

As you might suspect, moving to Montana was a big risk for me because it meant I would be giving myself more of a chance to enjoy what I had created. Geographically and emotionally, it was far removed from what I had grown up with. In a different way, however, I had taken this risk before. The fact that I had changed careers a number of times—from professor to therapist to consultant—also represented breaks with the past. My grandfather was a tailor and my father was a dentist for almost all of their adult lives.

Each generation escalates the level of risk, and our children are no exception. As they move further and further away from basic survival issues—from the literal *familiar* of each day being a struggle—they can take greater risks because lives are no longer at stake. Our children have been exposed to far more than I was—our eldest son has established himself in a successful career without the benefit of a college education; our middle son has studied in countries that were closed to the West during most of my adult life; and our youngest child goes to a private school and as an adolescent has traveled all over the world. This exposure to vast amounts of information, combined with his distance from my grandparents' survivalist mentality, allows him to push the risk envelope. He has chosen not to excel academically; he's risking having more obstacles in his search for a satisfying career because he won't have academic credentials to open doors. It would have been much more familiar (and easier) to follow in my footsteps. At the same time, he's also chosen to reproduce one aspect of our familial *familiar:* He's going to *struggle* to prove himself in the world without the advantages that top grades confer.

In one sense, every one of our children has responded to generational messages to which we also responded. In sometimes subtle and covert ways, we've all been encouraged to rebel. My grandparents would never have been able to embark on their journey to this country if someone hadn't given them the message that they didn't have to put up with persecution and poverty. My father received a similar message; otherwise he would not have challenged the status quo and enrolled as the only Jew in his dental school class. That same message prompted me to be a public figure who creates a great deal of controversy by attacking accepted (and sometimes treasured) notions about our culture. Our sons are responding to the message Arleah and I sent: "Challenge everything, and if you see something wrong, speak up because we'll hold you accountable for it."

HOW THESE GENERATIONAL MESSAGES
IMPACT OUR LIVES

It would be easy to deal with these messages if they were clear, direct, and written on a tablet handed down from one generation to the next. In reality, the messages you receive are often mixed and covert. It's worth the effort to decipher their meaning. They offer you another way to identify and frame the personal issues that are affecting your work.

For instance, the odds are great that some generational message is responsible in part for prompting you to read this. This book is about change and growth and doing better in your life. If you didn't receive a message encouraging you to change, grow, and do better, you would be engaged in some non-growth activity at this moment rather than reading this book. The more aware you are of what messages have been handed down, the better able you are to grieve the losses and take the risks that will help you grow.

Growing up, we often receive two types of messages:

1. *"Stay with what you know, with what is familiar."*
2. *"Don't put up with that, you can do better."*

It's difficult to argue with the first message. It's the message that leads to four generations of doctors (or ministers or teachers or lawyers). It encourages people to live in the same place and in the same way as earlier generations. This is a very human message; it recommends you play it safe, make it easier on yourself, and be comfortable. If this is the only message you listen to, however, you'll never do any better. The second message says, "Shoot for the stars"; it embodies most parents' dreams that their children will have a better life than they have. From an Internal Frontier perspective, the key is to be aware of both messages, act on the second one, and understand there's a price to be paid for doing so. That price is a loss that must be grieved. Once you grieve it, you will be in a better position to create a new *familiar*.

Arleah and I have made a number of decisions in our lives that have entailed acting on the "you can do better" message, and which have resulted in loss. What we've lost is a rich, extended-family tradition. When my parents were growing up, sixty family members lived within a short distance in the same area of Chicago. They were a necessary support group, and they facilitated survival. Growing up, I derived strength and inspiration from the extended family around me. The decision to move to Montana, as well as other, less dramatic decisions, robbed us of this extended-family experience. Sometimes it's sad and lonely to be separated from it, especially during holidays, and we continue to grieve that loss. But we also created new holiday traditions for our immediate family, which often involve coordinating travel for all of us to some unique place on the planet.

If we weren't aware of the price we paid for our decisions and grieved the losses that resulted, we would put a governor on our growth. We would be so sad and lonely that we might say, "Never again will we do something like this," and rob ourselves of future opportunities. The same thing has happened professionally. When I chose to change careers—as I've done a number of times—I needed to grieve each career as I left it behind. If I had failed to do this, I would have spent most of my time blaming external factors for the necessary struggles in establishing myself in each career. Feeling the discomfort that came with each new role, I might sabotage my new work, resulting in clients complaining that they don't "understand" what I'm saying; this would reproduce my familiar feeling of being sad that others don't understand my view of the world.

By acting on the "do better" message and understanding the price we're going to pay for achieving more in our lives, we can continue to grow rather than get stuck in external blaming and reproducing the *familiar*.

FINDING YOUR GENERATIONAL MESSAGE

Struggle was the theme that ran through four generations of my family. The mixed message was:

1. *"Continue struggling by working much harder than you need to."*
2. *"You can do better by struggling less and enjoying what you've achieved more."*

The following questions might help you find the messages sent down through generations of your family and how you're responding to them:

- *What have you done in your life differently from the three preceding generations?*
- *As you look back on the past year, what in your life is different (for you, your spouse, and your children) from a typical year of your life when you were growing up?*
- *Looking back at your upbringing, who or what was the stabilizing force that kept your family together; what activities helped ensure that stability?*

- *Which people showed the greatest confidence in you as a child; who gave you the hardest time?*
- *How often do you see your extended family now as opposed to when you were a child?*
- *What have you lost or given up in your life; have you grieved it; have you created a new "tradition"; have you built a new familiar for yourself and your family?*

These questions are designed to help you think about and discuss what went on in your family and how it has affected you. It's another way to identify your familiar; it gives you a sense of what's comfortable for you and whether your current behaviors create comfort or discomfort in your life.

EVALUATING YOUR ANSWERS

While your answers to these questions will be unique, there are some common issues and concerns that often arise.

You should be aware of two warning signs in reviewing your answers. First, you might discover that you're living the same type of life as the previous generation. If this is the case, you're probably stuck or plateaued; you need to make a break with the past if you want to grow and develop as a person and at work. The other warning sign is that you're leading a different type of life from the one you grew up with but it's one that is empty of change, risk, relationships, and growth. Many people are leading very different lives from what was familiar to them as children, but the difference often has to do with their withdrawal. They haven't built new traditions, become involved in growth relationships, or established a new support system (to replace the old one of the extended family). They work and veg out, existing in a kind of limbo between the world of their past and the one that might be in their future.

What often stands out when people contrast their lives to those of previous generations is the notion of risk. The risks we need to take to break with our *familiar* are far more subtle than the ones our grandparents took. For them, risks could be life-threatening. We don't need to risk jail or starvation to break with our past.

At the same time, however, our grandparents generally didn't need to concern themselves with personal versus professional risk. We do. For instance, the idea of taking a professional risk is relatively easy to identify—telling your boss that if he doesn't consider moving you to a more growth-oriented position, you're leaving. Defining risk in your personal life is another matter. Let's say you've just moved to another city where you don't know anyone. It's a very different type of risk to take the first step toward a growth relationship; it's scary to approach someone and admit you're isolated and lonely in order to initiate a reciprocal, intimate relationship.

For this generation and certainly the next, unequal rates of growth in personal versus professional lives is a big issue. Maybe you find yourself growing by leaps and bounds professionally, but you are leading a very isolated personal life. You might be the type of person who is making a great deal of money, facing exciting work challenges daily, but lacks anyone with whom to share your wealth or experiences. As willing as you are to take risks professionally, you're unwilling to do so personally. Eventually, the no-growth personal life will impact the high-growth professional one. Personal stagnancy will make you depressed and impact your enthusiasm for work. You'll ask yourself: "What am I doing all this work for?"

A generation of workaholics would do well to examine the issues in previous generations' lives and how messages were handed down. They may well uncover a clue as to why they can take risks professionally but feel blocked in their attempts to establish healthy, productive relationships outside of work.

THE ROAD TO CLARITY RUNS THROUGH
THE INTERNAL FRONTIER

The impetus to examine familial messages and issues from our past as well as do the other self-discovery work described in this book is as powerful now as it has ever been. We are bombarded with information and new opportunities to explore. The Internet, the global marketplace, and the rapid pace of change all have contributed to an abundance and accessibility of knowledge and opportunities. Most of us are overwhelmed. We lose our ability to differentiate between the inconsequential decisions and the significant life choices. We turn down high-growth job offers and accept comfortable, low-growth positions. Sometimes we find it difficult to make any choice at all, paralyzed by an overwhelming amount of data and possibilities.

The Internal Frontier allows you to crystallize the issues that are really important. By identifying your *familiar*, you can cut through the mist of the past and deal with present realities. The *familiar* causes us to misperceive a comfortable job as a growth-oriented one; it makes us mistake a terrific opportunity as "wrong for us" because it makes us uncomfortable. Once you're in touch with what's *familiar* for you, you can clarify your decision-making.

For instance, you might have grown up feeling as if you never made an impact on anyone in your life. As a child, your parents and siblings placed you on the periphery of family life, and you felt that nothing you did ever affected other family members. As an adult, you reproduce this *familiar*, placing yourself in situations where you manage to avoid having any sort of impact, especially at work. You relegate yourself to the role of a functionary, doing tasks but ensuring that you don't take on any sort of meaningful management role. Over time, however, you engage in a process of self-discovery that helps you become aware of this *familiar* and its origins. You determine that your vision is to be a person of great impact. With this awareness and determination, you're able to make good, fast decisions about job opportunities. You're aware that any position that allows you to have impact makes you uncomfortable. Rather than running from that discomfort, however, you'll run toward it, knowing that it fits with your vision. It also helps you steer clear of opportunities that offer a great deal of siz-zle—nice salary, perks, prestigious job title—but little or no impact on the lives of others.

Our increasing ability to obtain information elec-tronically about any subject under the sun is also over-whelming people with choices—choices that the Internal Frontier helps people make. You can now choose to do your taxes yourself by obtaining a piece of software or using sites on the Internet. You can access amazing amounts of information, support groups, and expert advice about how to start your own business. If you're a doctor, you can go on-line and read about a thousand new ongoing research studies and alternative therapies that might affect how you treat patients. If you're a parent, you'll find tremendous electronic resources that could make it possible for you to home-school your child.

All of this "instant expertise" forces you to make innumerable decisions that previous generations rarely had to consider. The pressure to decide causes great stress, and many people become distressed because they don't know how to make effective decisions. Or they simply make the wrong decisions. Without information about ourselves, we go from one bad choice to another. Like kids in a candy store, we look at a new job and say, "That looks good; I think I'll take it." What often makes it look good is our *familiar;* it offers comfort rather than growth, stasis rather than change.

People who have explored their Internal Frontiers may not find these decisions easy, but they find them manageable and make ones that help them lead increasingly effective, productive careers. It also gives them the ability to form relationships that ease the burden of all this decision-making; they become skilled at forming relationships in which they give and receive feedback that helps them clarify their values, create new *familiars,* and simplify their choices by being able to act on their feelings and self-knowledge.

A MORE MEANINGFUL, FULFILLING LIFE

Throughout this book, the focus has been on how dealing with personal issues can put you on the path of professional growth and development. It's important to remember, however, that you don't have to sacrifice meaningful work in exchange for growth and development. Many of us are under the impression that we have to choose between a satisfying, meaningful career and one that offers financial rewards. The Internal Frontier is a process that helps people achieve both.

The confusion about meaningful work arises because we often equate comfort with fulfillment and happiness. Again, this goes back to our generational messages. Most of us grew up hearing stories about how terrible things were, with the implication that they could stay that way for the foreseeable future. Even though we're now far removed from that survivalist imperative, we continue attempting to put more distance between ourselves and the terrible discomfort our parents or grandparents experienced. Our goal becomes to reach a point in our lives where there is no discomfort. The ideal job, therefore, is one where we never have to worry or take on new and scary assignments that cause us anxiety. In other words, the ideal job is a no-growth one. In this situation, the ungrieved past comes to dominate the present and the future.

What's meaningful always involves a certain amount of discomfort, alternating with a certain amount of deep satisfaction when goals are achieved. In a sense, the discomfort is a measure for what's meaningful. We've all heard stories about people who became deathly ill, and when they recovered they talked about how they had a new appreciation for what's important in their lives. Discomfort, like disappointment, helps us judge what we should focus on. It's a sign that we're in unfamiliar territory and need to explore it. It signals a challenge that's satisfying to meet.

Leading a meaningful life isn't about owning the biggest house or the most expensive car, though they can be by-products of leading this type of life. While these luxuries can be satisfying, they can be comforting in the same way that an anesthetic relieves pain. They dull our senses to all the challenges and growth opportunities out there. They keep us in our pain-free *familiar*.

What I hope this book helps you do is move away from the unproductive *familiar* and focus your life on something that is tremendously gratifying and involving. Instead of doing what is easy, you'll choose to do something that fosters continuous growth and change.

AN EQUAL OPPORTUNITY PROCESS

At this point in my life, I've heard every excuse about why people can't explore the Internal Frontier. Some say they're "not ready" to do so; they haven't reached a point in their lives where they want to investigate these internal issues. Others protest that they don't have the time. There are also people who scoff at the very notion that anything in their personal life could impact their professional one.

But perhaps the most common objection to this process is that they lack the "freedom" necessary for self-exploration. People explain that they labor under real-world constraints; that their employers would never endorse such things as accountability groups and the types of trusting, reciprocal relationships the process calls for; that the demands of their jobs are overwhelming and that they don't have the time or energy to devote to "personal stuff."

If these excuses come to your mind as well, recognize that they are easily overcome. As nice as it would be if your organization endorsed this methodology or if you already had an Internal Frontier process in place, you can do this work on your own. The only thing necessary is to establish at least one relationship in which you give and receive feedback, express feelings, and establish accountability—

a relationship that can be formed outside the work environment. It doesn't require a huge investment of time, and it doesn't depend on the approval of a supervisor.

At this point, you probably know what lies behind the excuses: an avoidance of the discomfort that comes with confronting these emotionally charged issues. You need to take a risk to surface the elemental disappointment from your childhood. It hurts to talk about how you felt then and the negative behaviors it's producing now. Letting go and giving up certain parts of yourself is sad, and it's a sadness that needs to be grieved. In other words, don't think that you're odd or unusual if you've resisted personal-growth approaches in the past.

On the other hand, there are great rewards for those who plunge into the wilderness of the Internal Frontier. Throughout this book, I've discussed the personal–professional connection, and how people who make it achieve highly ambitious work and career goals. Let me leave you with one other benefit of creating this linkage in your life.

People who address their internal issues have a huge impact on their environments. Personal transformation produces extraordinary influence and attraction. A high percentage of individuals who have gone through our Fifth Wave programs have become leaders in their organizations. Other people resonate to their courage, trust, directness, and ability to express their feelings. People who are experiencing continuous and phenomenal rates of growth attract everyone's attention, and it's clear that they're going places.

My hope is that this book will help you grow and develop in ways that may not have seemed possible in the past and that now seem limitless. The belief in your own capacity to make different choices—to not leave your life to chance—is a gift only you can give to yourself.

ACKNOWLEDGMENTS

A s I indicated in the introduction, this book is a collaborative effort, but not in the traditional sense. Arleah, Jim, Rick, and I did not sit down together through a series of meetings and write a group book. All of us, with extensive experience in working on committees and with teams, know what that would have produced. In addition, all four of us are strong and opinionated personalities, and we would have had a wonderful and energetic time challenging and confronting each other, while producing as much as a Senate white paper on truth in government.

Arleah, Jim, and Rick all contributed significantly to a number of specific chapters, but their contributions to the total body of knowledge in this book is inestimable. We all have very special relationships, and they have enriched me intellectually, professionally, and personally beyond description.

Arleah's ability to cut through interpersonal clutter and penetrate fortress-like defenses is unparalleled in my life. No one cuts to the core of one's emotional center, and no one can open up people who have been sealed up and shut down all their lives, like Arleah can. She has been my life companion, best friend, valued challenger, and most ardent supporter for the past twenty years. We have raised children together, created our personal vision through our home in Montana, and have had the rare privilege of working together professionally. I cannot imagine life without her, and have only vague memories of life before her.

Jim Blackburn is a natural and perpetual teacher. I don't know that I've ever seen Jim do anything without teaching something to someone. Every life experience that Jim has (or any of us, for that matter) becomes an opportunity to create what Jim calls a "learning event." He seems to have an inherent ability to structure exercises and processes around knowledge and observations that result in experiences that change people's behavior, and fundamentally impact their lives.

Rick Kremer is an astounding dynamo of implementation. At middle age, no one has more energy and focus than Rick, other than perhaps Mick Jagger and the Rolling Stones (not coincidentally, Rick's all-time favorite rock group). Rick has the ability to take interesting, provocative, and cutting-edge concepts, and give them form, substance, and organizational life. While others endlessly debate and puzzle over what to do, Rick makes things happen and creates fundamental and long-lasting change in organizations and individuals.

My first structured journey into my own Internal Frontier began in my mid-twenties, when I sought help with a troubled marriage that eventually failed. Over the course of the next few years, I met and worked with Robert Mungerson, an extraordinary therapist and one of the most remarkable human beings I've ever encountered. His intuitive capabilities verged on the supernatural. He was so finely attuned to his own internal processes that he resonated to other people's feelings with an accuracy and specificity that often scared and threatened people. It took me a while to get used to the emotional vulnerability one felt in his presence, but once I did, I embarked on my first real journey into self-exploration and growth. Mungerson taught me two lessons that have stayed with and grounded me my entire life. The first was that nothing happens to people by accident. Individuals always play a role in shaping their destinies, and always exercise choices in creating the situations in which they find themselves. The second lesson was that feelings, rather than intellect, are a much more accurate instrument for locating the truth. Mungerson was intellectually brilliant, and helped me make sense of the jumble of psychological concepts I had been exposed to in my formal education and training. But his brilliance only came into play after his instincts and intuition pointed him in the right direction. He taught me to pay attention to my gut; to react and respond to what my feelings were telling me. For that, I am extremely grateful. Unfortunately, our relationship was my first experience in profound loss. Mungerson died an early and tragic death at the peak of his career and the zenith of his impact on a number of us lucky enough to have known and worked with him.

My professional life, as has been my historical pattern, has undergone profound change in the last few years. I became a part of a high-growth public company, became a member of its board of directors, and learned an enormous amount about both from a unique inside vantage point. This all came about as a result of meeting Ted Schwartz.

Ted and I met in Johannesburg, South Africa, in February 1995, at a YPO (Young Presidents Organization) University. It was a life-changing experience for both of us. He is the founder and CEO of APAC Teleservices, and is a legend in the outsourcing and telemarketing industry. In addition, Ted is a true business visionary. He not only sees what's coming down the road, he already has the vehicle constructed in his mind for the upcoming drive. As soon as we met, it was clear that we shared a commitment to individual growth and learning, and that we both saw the future viability and success of the business community intimately tied to the development of people. Ted has been unwavering in his support of my work and my vision, and I am deeply grateful to him. Arleah and I greatly value our relationship with him and Chris, and look forward to growing and expanding it in the future.

Fortunately, one of the things that hasn't changed in my life is my relationship with Bob Kerrigan, the general agent for Northwestern Mutual Life in Los Angeles. Over the past fifteen years, Bob and I have developed a very unique and extraordinarily valued relationship, combining a close personal friendship and a professional connection that has allowed me to see my concepts and ideas articulated and manifested in a living, breathing organization that develops and sustains highly successful people. I can always depend on Bob to help me when I'm struggling with a conceptual or personal issue. His clarity and his feedback are unerringly on target, and I always leave our all-too-infrequent interactions re-energized and refocused.

For Arleah and me, two individuals have added immensely to our quality of life over the past few years. They are Pam Brauer, my professional assistant, and Mary Krager, Arleah's professional assistant as well as our personal assistant.

Pam makes my professional life possible. There is no way I could carry off the multiplicity of involvements that characterize a typical week in my work life without her. She is not simply well-organized; it is more than that. She doesn't miss a thing. Nothing slips through the cracks. Additionally, it is rare that a few weeks go by without my getting feedback from a client or an associate as to what a pleasure it is to deal with her.

But what I most value about our relationship is that she believes in what we do in our practice, and she walks our talk in her work with our clients and within the Institute. I can depend on Pam, without exception, to deliver on her accountabilities, and to hold me and others to delivering on ours. She truly understands the concept of making a commitment, and models the height of professionalism in honoring hers.

Mary, in her work with Arleah and myself, has truly created a new, cutting-edge role in our culture. She makes it possible for us to survive and thrive in our almost totally "virtual" lifestyle, by enabling us to pursue a global business practice while reaping the emotional and spiritual benefits of living in one of the most spectacular and beautiful places in the world. Her work combines the skill sets of a traditional housewife, bookkeeper, property manager, caterer/chef, administrative assistant, community liaison, tour guide/outfitter, social director, adviser, and confidante. She has helped us redefine "family," and has made an invaluable contribution to the quality of life of ourselves, our children, our friends, and our professional associates. Both Arleah and I feel privileged to have Mary and Pam in our lives, and thankful that they continue to put up with our constant and consistent needs, "feedback," and expectations to grow.

Morrie Shechtman